SOOTHING THE MENTAL STORM

The Ultimate Guide to Breaking Free from the Cage of Excessive Thinking. New Techniques and Practical Tips for Self-Improvement to Free the Mind and Return to a Peaceful Life.

Amos Lloyd

Amos Lloyd

Copyright © 2024 Amos Lloyd

All rights reserved.

This document is intended to provide accurate and reliable information on the subject matter discussed. The publication is sold with the understanding that the publisher is not obligated to provide officially licensed or otherwise certified accounting services. If legal or professional advice is required, a qualified professional should be consulted.

Reproducing, duplicating, or transmitting any part of this document in electronic or printed form is illegal. Recording or storing this publication is strictly prohibited without the written consent of the publisher. All rights reserved.

The information provided in this document is stated to be true and consistent. However, the reader is solely responsible for the use or misuse of any policy, process, or guidance contained herein. Under no circumstances shall the publisher be held liable for any legal issues, damages, or financial loss arising from the information in this document, whether directly or indirectly.

The information in this document is solely for general informational purposes and is not associated with any warranties. The trademarks used here are for illustration purposes only and belong to their respective owners, who are not affiliated with this document.

Summary

INTRODUCTION 8

CHAPTER 1 THOUGHTS: WHAT THEY ARE AND HOW THEY ARISE IN OUR MINDS. 14

1.1 WHAT IS THOUGHT? 14

1.2 FUNDAMENTAL BASES OF THOUGHT 17

   Definition 17

   Representation 18

   Process 18

1.3 CLASSIFICATION OF THOUGHTS 19

   Deductive reasoning 19

   What are the characteristics of deductive reasoning? 20

   It involves logical argumentation 21

   Assume the premises to be true 22

   It does not produce new information 22

   The conclusion is proper if the premises are true 22

   Is exposed to lies 23

   Examples of reasoning based on deduction 24

   Syllogism 24

   Modus tollendo tollens 24

   Modus ponendo ponens 25

   Untrue premises leading to falsehoods 25

   Illogical reasoning leading to falsehoods 25

1.4 INDUCTIVE REASONING 26

   What is inductive reasoning? 27

  Characteristics of inductive reasoning 27

  Individual premise 28

  Conclusion 28

  Tendentially expansive 28

  Fallible 28

  Non-qualifying 29

  Example of inductive reasoning 30

  Why is inductive reasoning so critical? 31

1.5 CREATIVE THINKING 32

  What is creative thinking? 32

  Characteristics of creative thinking 34

  Research 37

  Incubation 37

  Enlightenment 38

  Verification 38

  What is expected from creative thinking? 38

  Examples of creative thinking 39

  The importance of creative thinking 40

1.6 CRITICAL THINKING 41

  What is critical thinking? 41

  Stages of critical thinking 42

  Characteristics of critical thinking 43

  Examples of critical thinking 44

  Importance 44

  Understanding thoughts 45

CHAPTER 2 THE SIDEWALK OF EXCESSIVE THOUGHTS 49

2.1 Why do we overthink? 49

2.2 The quantity of thoughts in our minds can be a problem, but even more so, the quality of these thoughts. 52

2.3 Causes of overthinking 54

Potential causes of overthinking 56

Parenting and beliefs 56

Desire to make the right decision 60

Handling problems responsibly 61

Stressful situations 62

CHAPTER 3 CHARACTERISTICS OF OVERTHINKING 65

3.1 They begin to relate their decisions to their fears 66

3.2 They Usually Need Approval from Others 68

3.3 They are prone to pessimism 70

3.4 They Create Imaginary Scenarios in Their Mind 71

3.5 They believe the rest of the world is angry with them. 72

3.6 They tend to be quite emotional. 73

3.7 They tend to worry excessively about the people around them. 76

3.8 They are prone to turning their condition into an addiction. ... 77

3.9 What are the consequences of overthinking? 78

How do I know if I am overthinking? 78

Your mind doesn't stop 80

Is it like your mind never stops working? Are you having trouble unwinding because you're constantly thinking and worrying? 80

You're not alone if you've ever laid in bed wondering, "Why can't I fall asleep?" 80

There are many reasons for a frantic or busy mind 80

Stress is a usual suspect when you can't stop thinking 81

Stress causes your body to release cortisol, which helps you stay alert. This means that your brain also stays alert, even when you don't want it to. 81

You can't relax or sleep because cortisol can make you feel anxious 81

It's possible to keep thinking the same things over and over again without ever finding a way to fix the issue or worry. 81

It can feel like your brain has been hijacked. Even when you realize you're overthinking, recognise that it's unproductive, and try to push the thoughts away. They won't stop. 81

You suffer from insomnia 81

Some situations aren't easily forgotten 83

The brain holds onto embarrassing moments 84

Too much doubt 86

CHAPTER 4 ESCAPING THE CAGE OF EXCESSIVE THOUGHTS 88

What are the first steps to stop overthinking? 89

4.1 RECOGNISE PATTERNS 89

Notice if situations become repetitive 94

4.2 IDENTIFYING THE CAUSE OF DISCOMFORT 95

4.3 IDENTIFYING OUR RESPONSIBILITIES 97

4.4 GATHERING THE INFORMATION FROM THE PREVIOUS POINTS 98

Reprogramming the way we think about ourselves 100

4.5 REDEFINING YOURSELF EVERY DAY 107

4.6 CREATE A POSITIVE MANTRA 109

4.7 BEING PRESENT IN THE MOMENT 111

4.8 AVOID MULTITASKING 114

4.9 PUTTING AN END TO LIMITING THOUGHTS 115

4.10 DON'T TALK ABOUT THE PAST 118

What should we do, then, to forget the past? 120

4.11 INCLUDE MEDITATION IN YOUR DAILY ACTIVITIES 129

Guided meditation 131

Meditating alone 132

4.12 FINDING SOLUTIONS TO OUR PROBLEMS 134

4.13 HOW TO PROACTIVELY COMBAT NEGATIVE THOUGHTS? 135

Question 1: Is the thought I'm having real, meaning, is there evidence to support it? 136

Question 2: Is this thought helpful? 137

Question 3: Do I feel good about this thought? 137

CONCLUSION **140**

You are not weak or flawed. 146

FINAL ACKNOWLEDGEMENTS **149**

Introduction

Nowadays, many of us get too caught up in our thoughts, often finding ourselves stuck in the endless spiral of "what ifs" that come and go with life.

What if I cannot afford it? What if they do not share my preferences? What if this change makes matters worse?

In general, "overthinking" refers to the repetitive and unproductive thought process. Research has generally distinguished between rumination on the past and present and worry about the future.

Understanding the factors that can contribute to this problem will help you take steps to overcome it.

Fear is a major contributor to overthinking. The fear of failure, rejection and disappointment leads to excessive thinking.

Our brains are amazing at processing information, making conscious and unconscious choices up to 35,000 times per day. Getting caught up in analyzing every potential outcome can lead to unnecessary worry and decision paralysis.

Overthinking has a lot in common with solving problems, so it's easy to see why. However, they are not the same thing.

Problem-solving involves asking questions in order to find an answer or implement a solution. Overthinking occurs when you focus on possibilities and pitfalls without any real intention of solving the problem. It's possible that there's no real issue or conceivable issue at all.

Your ability to think is one of your greatest strengths. Our brains have evolved to produce complex thoughts, enabling us to process information, solve problems, plan and learn from our past. Thinking has empowered us to create complex societies and advance as a species over time.

If you find yourself continually pondering the same issue without finding a resolution, you might be overthinking. Let's consider a specific example of someone who overthinks and distorts reality:

A couple has a son who excels in school and is polite, athletic and obedient.

The mother recently changed jobs, which gave her more time to spend at home with her son and consequently more time to think.

She begins to contemplate the past and worries about the future, developing strange anxieties about her son's behaviour,

From that moment on, the mother starts imagining that her son is hiding something from her and starts following him after school without his knowledge.

The same routine repeats each day for some time: the mother imagines catastrophic scenarios where her son engages in irresponsible behaviour with his friend after school. One day, the son doesn't go home after school but heads to another area with a friend.

The mother tries to follow them but loses track of them, so she returns home to wait for him for questioning.

When the boy returns, he immediately goes to his room after confirming to his mother that he went to study in a small square with his friend.

The next day, the same situation occurs, and the exhausted mother admits she doesn't trust him or believe what he says.

On the third day, overwhelmed by negative thoughts, she follows him to the end and gets out of the car to trail him.

At that moment, the son and his friend take their books from their backpacks and sit in the square to study.

The son did not lie to her, but her anxieties had distorted her perception of reality.

Anxiety is a powerful emotion that can wreak havoc on our minds and bodies; it's a feeling of unease or dread about something we can't control or predict. Uncertainty about the future, even regarding a simple outcome, can fuel anxiety and stress.

When we experience anxiety, our thoughts tend to focus on the worst-case scenario, which causes us to overthink.

Let's analyze the story of the mother and son. We realize that, driven by anxiety, she began to create negative scenarios in her mind, imagining that her son was putting himself in danger and lying to her.

Obviously, to the anxiety-ridden mother, her son's behaviour seemed to confirm her worries and catastrophic thoughts.

This state of hyper-vigilance can lead to overthinking, as our minds fixate on worst-case scenarios.

Overthinking can have a negative impact on how you interact with the world around you. It can hinder your ability to make essential decisions and enjoy the present moment while depleting the energy required to tackle daily stresses.

Furthermore, if you often dwell on the past or worry excessively about the future, negative thought patterns can harm your mental and physical well-being. From a mental health perspective, anxiety can affect your ability to handle everyday challenges, while depression can lead to feelings of sadness, isolation, and emptiness.

It's not always possible to handle this situation alone, so consulting professionals is necessary. Keep in mind that a generalized anxiety disorder can lead to high blood pressure and poor cardiovascular health, whereas a depressive state can lead to a heart attack or a suicide attempt.

Even though this phenomenon has existed in the past, modernity has improved the mind's ability to handle various situations. As people discovered their capabilities, they began to reflect more on the processes used to solve problems and make decisions. In today's modern world, we are constantly bombarded by social media, phones, and digital tools, which overwhelm us with information and stimuli, leading us to think more and more.

The first step in overcoming overthinking is understanding the causes. Identifying the factors that cause excessive thinking can ease tension, control anxieties, and alter thought patterns.

Practicing and being patient can help you relax and have a great life.

Let's look at how thoughts and overthinking evolve.

Chapter 1
Thoughts: What they are and how they arise in our minds.

1.1 What is thought?

Thinking is an activity expressed through creating archetypes, concepts, awareness, imagination, dreams, judgment, and opinions, shaping the world.

There are many definitions of thought, but we can define it as an action performed by the mind, whether conscious or unconscious, that results in the creation of certain "outputs" such as criticism, goals, judgments, and imagination. In other words, everything the mind creates is considered a thought, regardless of whether it is logical, creative, abstract, or rational. Thought mediates between internal activity and external stimuli.

The term "thinking" in everyday language encompasses a variety of psychological activities. At times, it is used to express a "tendency to believe," often with incomplete confidence ("I think it will rain, but I'm not sure"). Occasionally, it signifies the level of attention ("I performed it without thinking") or the state of consciousness, particularly when referring to an external factor ("I was reminded of my grandmother"). Psychologists have traditionally defined thinking as an intellectual effort to find an answer to a question or to solve a practical problem.

The psychology of mental processes deals with activities similar to those usually associated with an inventor, a mathematician or a chess player. However, psychologists have not settled on a single definition or characterization of thinking. For some, thinking involves modifying "cognitive structures" Some people see it as internal problem-solving behaviour, while others see it as perceptual representations of the world or parts of it.

In the past, people connected thinking to conscious experiences. However, as researchers in psychology developed the scientific study of behaviour (e.g., behaviourism), they recognised the limitations of using introspection as a data source. Since then, psychologists have thought of thoughts as things that happen when two things happen together. These events include input (present and past stimuli) and output (responses, such as bodily movements and speech). Many psychologists use these intervening variables to understand the highly complex network of associations between stimulus conditions and responses, which would otherwise be challenging to analyse. Others focus on identifying the cognitive (or mental) structures that consciously or unconsciously guide a person's observable behavior.

Subvocalizing, which involves silently combining linguistic elements, is considered a form of thinking. Early experiments suggested that there is often electrical activity in the muscles of the thinker's throat during thinking. However, later use of electromyographic equipment clarified that muscle activity does not cause thinking; it simply supports the brain's activities during challenging intellectual tasks.

It's crucial to remember that every decision we make results from our thought process, which is influenced by our perception, knowledge, and ability to absorb information and experiences.

1.2 Fundamental bases of thought

As we have read in previous pages, thinking is an essential and adaptable human process.

It helps us solve problems, learn new information and understand concepts. Thinking involves learning, memory, and mental organization, giving us the ability to comprehend information better and recall it later.

Although there are different types of thinking or ways of thinking, the structure that underlies it is based on three key elements that influence our minds:

- Definition
- Representation
- Process

Definition

Whenever we hear a word, our mind automatically connects it with an object or an image. Our brain associates a word with all the data it's gathered.

Let's consider a specific example of a definition: When we think about animals, our mind automatically goes to a generic concept. Despite the fact that there are numerous distinct species, the term 'animals' encompasses them all.

Our mind tends to associate this word with a generalized concept because of this.

Representation

Fundamentally, our thoughts are maps that represent and correspond to things our brain has perceived through our senses, felt through our emotions, or formed as a plan of action. Thoughts can be fleeting or may later consolidate into memories. Changes in neural connections in neural pathways encode memory as well. Sensory perceptions and memories are physical representations.

At this stage, our mind makes in-depth associations, shaping thoughts.

Through representation, humans have also been able to create language.

Process

It is a cognitive activity that involves the mental capacity to understand and perform various functions related to human experience. These mental operations enable us to solve problems, make decisions, and generate and assess new ideas.

Engaging in thought processes also helps us gain insight into our feelings and preferences.

Developing and applying these cognitive operations can enhance our ability to connect and communicate effectively by enabling us to understand situations and the frameworks that influence our behaviour.

1.3 Classification of thoughts

Our minds produce various thoughts: some are more important, while others are of little use, and most help us make decisions in the face of life's small and significant challenges.

One way to gain better control over your thoughts is to become familiar with them and learn to distinguish each thought your brain generates.

While it's true that many thoughts appear in your mind involuntarily, becoming aware of them can allow you to make an effort to gain greater control over them.

Deductive reasoning

Deductive reasoning, also known as deduction, involves analysing valid forms of argumentation to draw conclusions that are implicit in their premises. Different types of deductive argumentation can be used to solve problems or to reason. In conditional reasoning, the thinker must draw a conclusion based on a conditional proposition, such as "if... then". The conditional proposition "If today is Monday, then I will attend the cooking class" and the statement "Today is Monday" can be used to draw the conclusion: "I will attend the cooking class today." Two types of valid inference can be derived from a conditional proposition. In an argument known as modus ponens, the statement affirms the conditional's antecedent, and the conclusion affirms the consequent.

In modus tollens, the statement denies the conditional result, and the conclusion denies the antecedent. Deductive reasoning starts with a general assumption, applies logic, and then verifies that logic to conclude. The conclusion will be valid if the premises are true with this approach. We can reach a final idea to work on by thinking like this.

What are the characteristics of deductive reasoning?

Like other forms of thought, deductive reasoning has specific characteristics. Below, we will examine the main ones.

It involves logical argumentation

Deductive logical arguments begin with valid arguments that demonstrate the truth of mathematical proofs and information.

To determine if a question falls into this category, one must refer to scientific definitions such as:

- Modus ponens.
- Modus tollens.
- Syllogism.

This means that if the premises (letter A) are correct, the conclusion (letter B) will also be accurate.

It's important to note that if the initial hypotheses are correct, the conclusion will also be accurate.

When discussing logical argument, we use mechanisms to confirm or refute truths and information.

The argument, which has a defined structure, follows a specific order, making the order more important than the content.

Assume the premises to be true

Deductive reasoning involves starting with general premises and then using them to arrive at a specific conclusion by analysing the various variables involved.

For instance, if you enter a store and notice that the clothes are expensive, you can deduce that the store is too costly for you.

This example illustrates that deductive reasoning must begin with the certainty that one or more pieces of information are valid; otherwise, a distinct conclusion cannot be reached.

It does not produce new information

Deductive reasoning does not generate new information; it uses true premises to support arguments and reach conclusions without requiring additional information.

The conclusion is proper if the premises are true.

The fundamental characteristics of deductive reasoning can be summarised as follows:

- The conclusion must logically follow from the premises

- if the premises are true and the conclusion logically follows from them, then the conclusion will also be valid

- the conclusion can always be traced back to the premises, although sometimes it is explicitly stated.

- It's important to note that in deductive reasoning, the focus is not on the argument behind the premises but on the fact that if the premises are true, the conclusion will also be valid.

Is exposed to lies

As previously mentioned, deductive thinkers do not assess the truthfulness of premises or focus on their content. Consequently, if the reasoning is based on false or partially true premises, it will lead to untruthful conclusions. The same situation can occur when there is uncertainty about the validity of the premises. Flawed reasoning and incorrect conclusions may result if the truthfulness of the premises is still being determined.

Examples of reasoning based on deduction

Deductive reasoning can be used to test deductions using syllogism, modus ponens, and modus tollens. Let's take a closer look at each of them.

Syllogism

Syllogism is the simplest of 3 types of deductive reasoning. The syllogism says, "If A=B and B=C, then A=C." Two separate clauses are connected. Another creative example: a puma is a cat, and cats are mammals. Therefore, pumas are mammals.

Modus tollendo tollens

Modus ponens is a form of deductive reasoning where a conditional statement is presented and proven true by providing evidence for both the antecedent and the consequent. For instance, if we have the conditional statement "If someone is a Lakers player, then they are between 21 and 31 years old", and we also have the premise "Mario Rossi is a Lakers player." Mario Rossi must be between the ages of 21 and 31.

Modus ponendo ponens

Modus tollens is the opposite of a modus ponens. While modus ponens affirms a conditional statement, modus tollens refutes it. For instance, in the event of a fever, it is imperative that your temperature exceeds 37 Celsius degrees. If your temperature is below 37 degrees, then you do not have a fever.

Other examples of deductive thinking include:

Untrue premises leading to falsehoods

- All men always wear jeans.
- Jesus is a man.
- Therefore, Luca always wears jeans.

Illogical reasoning leading to falsehoods

- If a girl is crying, it is because she is hungry.
- A girl is crying.
- Therefore, this girl must be hungry.

It's important to remember that reaching a false conclusion is easy when the premises are incorrect or partially incorrect. Deductive thinking is commonly used, and failing to verify the validity of the premises can mislead many people, leading them to inaccurate conclusions.

Let's proceed with the analysis of other types of thinking.

1.4 Inductive reasoning

Many aspects of problem-solving involve inductive reasoning or induction. Induction is a method for reasoning from specific situations to general principles, from the past to the present, or from the observed to the unseen. It is impossible for the conclusion to be false if the premises are true, while deductive inferences guarantee the truth of their conclusions. Inductive reasoning includes causal inference, categorical inference, and logical inference.

One can conclude that something is the cause of something else by evaluating it. Hearing the sound of a piano may lead to the conclusion that someone is playing a piano. Although this conclusion may be possible, it is not certain that the sounds came from an electronic synthesizer. (Also see induction, problem of.)

One judges whether something is a member of a specific category in a categorical inference. For example, upon seeing an animal one has never seen before, a person with limited knowledge of dogs may be confident that they see a dog but less sure about the specific breed.

Analogical reasoning involves applying what one has learned in one field to another. Aristotle offered two possible logical inferences: "As A is to B, so C is to D" and "As A is in B, so C is in D." Analogical inference involves applying the results of a known situation to a new or unknown situation. However, a risk in this approach can occur if the two conditions are too dissimilar to warrant an analogous comparison.

What is inductive reasoning?

In 1938, Leon Thurstone identified inductive thinking as a type of thought based on the analysis of specific observations. This type of analysis leads to general conclusions (inductive reasoning vs. deductive reasoning).

Inductive reasoning is a way of thinking that people use in everyday situations.

Characteristics of inductive reasoning

Inductive reasoning begins with a specific premise and then extends to form a generalized conclusion; with this type of thinking, the conclusion could be false even if the premises are true.

Individual premise

Starting from a specific premise allows us to have a clear opinion.

Conclusion

In this case, the conclusion is not implicit in the premises; even if the premises are true, the conclusion may not be.

We can say that inductive reasoning is:

Tendentially expansive

Unlike deductive reasoning, the content in the premises is significant, and thanks to the conclusion, we can gain new information that we didn't have before.

Fallible

It is not definitive since the conclusions are never certain, only possible.

Non-qualifying

Inductive reasoning is non-qualifying, as it is a bottom-up approach, in contrast to top-down deductive reasoning.

It is commonly used in fields such as experimentation and innovation, where we deal with possibilities rather than certainties. We gather information to support our arguments.

Deductive reasoning involves making inferences by moving from general premises to specific conclusions. You start with a idea and then make a prediction based on evidence. You collect data from numerous observations and use statistical tests to draw conclusions based on your hypothesis.

Inductive research is typically exploratory, as it involves developing theories through generalisations. Deductive research, on the other hand, tends to back up previous findings.

In some research studies, both inductive and deductive approaches are combined.

Example of inductive reasoning

Inductive generalisations use observations from a sample to draw conclusions about the population from which it comes.

Inductive generalisations are also known as enumeration induction.

Example: inductive generalisation

- Pink is the color of the flamingos.
- Every flamingo I have ever seen is pink.
- All flamingos must be pink.

Several criteria are used to evaluate inductive generalisations.

- A big sample is important for a solid set of observations.
- Random sampling methods allow you to generalize the results.
- Variety: your observations should have external validity.
- Counterexample: any observation that contradicts yours generalisation falsifies it.

Why is inductive reasoning so critical?

Inductive reasoning, **a process we all engage in daily**, often without even realising it, is the act of forming a generalisation based on a series of specific observations.

It's a tool we use to make sense of the world around us. However, it also supports the scientific approach, which serves as the foundation for undertaking investigations. Researchers collect data - specific observations - from which they form hypotheses - generalisations - that guide further research.

Let's distinguish between the main characteristics of inductive and deductive reasoning. The bottom-up reasoning of inductive reasoning begins with specific observations leading to a generalisation, while the top-down reasoning of deductive reasoning begins with general principles leading to particular conclusions.

Scientists have advanced human knowledge and fostered innovation thanks to inductive reasoning. Inductive reasoning is used to conduct scientific research within the framework of the scientific method. Researchers were unable to form hypotheses based on their observations without induction.

Hypotheses guide future research and the development of new theories, making inductive inference essential for scientific progress.

Furthermore, the inductive inferences we make daily, often without conscious effort, are incredibly useful for broadening our understanding of the world. By identifying patterns in our environment, we gain insights into how the world works and how we should behave. Something as simple as knowing that you can find the ingredients to make a sandwich in your refrigerator because that's where you found them the day before is an example of inductive reasoning.

1.5 Creative thinking

Creative thinkers explore multiple perspectives and possibilities, enabling them to pursue different paths of knowledge. Unlike deductive and inductive reasoning, creative thinking focuses on how we reprocess the information we receive.

What is creative thinking?

Creative thinking involves developing innovative solutions to problems. Creative thinkers brainstorm a large number of ideas and a variety of them.

Creative thinkers experiment with their ideas after brainstorming. They view ideas from multiple perspectives and examine how their solutions fit within the scope of their work. Creative thinkers are not afraid of taking risks and enjoy generating new ideas. They are a valuable asset for almost any workplace because of their ability to develop, test, and implement original solutions. At work, creative thinking can look like:

- Conducting an interactive brainstorming session to gather initial thoughts on a project.
- Evaluating an ongoing process and offering suggestions on how to improve it.
- Researching different ways to market a product and experimenting with new marketing channels.
- A new way to reach potential clients is being developed.
- Identifying a unique opportunity to promote the company's brand and creating a strategy.

The concept of creativity is not just a psychological aspect of education, but a cornerstone of societal progress. Creativity is the key to the advancement of any nation. Hence, in the contemporary era, forward-thinking nations are dedicated to nurturing creativity in their youth.

Creative individuals are born into diverse circumstances. History shows that many philosophers, poets, writers, and painters who were once labelled underperforming students and dropped out of school later created marvellous works.

The aforementioned definition emphasizes that creative thinking entails the ability to engage in original thinking, explore novel associations, engage in divergent thinking and behavior, and devise novel solutions to enduring issues. The thinking of a creative is dynamic, flexible, original and novel.

Creativity is a subjective trait. Not everyone is universally creative, but each person may have areas where their creativity shines and others where it may not be as pronounced.

Characteristics of creative thinking

Creative thinking has several key characteristics, which we will now list point by point:

- To be creative, a person should be well aware of the problems in their circumstances. A creative person always looks for new ways to solve problems.

- Dynamic thinking: creative people think creatively and dynamically. They are more adaptable and seek this adaptability through new combinations.

- Creativity means thinking in different ways and coming up with new ideas. This is shown in the work of great scientists, philosophers, and writers.

- Besides being divergent, creativity leads to practical outcomes. According to Bruner, a new idea brings immense pleasure to the thinker, as it impresses everyone. He believes creative products must be impressive. Thus, a creative person is deeply involved in their work.

- An essential aspect of creative thinking is being flexible in thought and behaviour and always ready to adopt new attitudes, ideas, or behaviours.

- Originality is a vital characteristic of creative thinking. Creative individuals embrace new ideas, attitudes, and methods without constraints.

- To achieve the traits of creative thinking mentioned above, a person should possess sufficient curiosity. Curiosity drives people to learn new things in any field and encourages them to try new methods.

- An ordinary person is often limited by their environment and immediate circumstances, whereas a creative person can surpass immediate circumstances and showcase originality in thoughts and actions.

- To find innovative solutions, it is important to look at the problem from a new angle. The subject of consideration should be new and valuable. Thinking should be divergent, highly motivated and coherent.

Doing research and practicing in relevant areas and materials will give you new ideas, help you think differently, and help you develop a valuable human trait called creativity.

Creative thinking involves several stages. According to a well-known theory, preparation is the first step in solving a problem. The next stage is incubation, where the individual freely considers possibilities without rigid preconceptions and logical constraints. Enlightenment occurs when the resources fall into place, leading to a definitive decision regarding the outcome or solution. The final stage is verification, which involves making minor adjustments to finalise the ideas in their final form.

Although the four stages are typically presented in a logical order, they can vary widely and unfold differently for each person. Many creative individuals achieve their goals by following unique strategies, and describing these approaches is essential. The preparation, incubation, enlightenment, and verification stages are typical among creative thinkers, but they don't guarantee a successful outcome. The results also hinge on an individual's possession of the necessary personality traits and abilities. Additionally, the quality of creative thinking is influenced by the creator's training. Creative thinking involves utilising internal resources to generate concrete outcomes. Early experiences and training significantly shape this process.

Let's look at each stage of creating more closely.

Research

Collect information and gather materials, find sources of inspiration, and obtain knowledge about the project or issue. This involves both internal processes (reflecting deeply to generate and engage with ideas) and external ones (venturing into the world to gather the required data, resources, materials, and expertise).

Incubation

In the next stage, the ideas and information gathered in the first stage are stored in the mind. New connections are formed as these ideas simmer. This incubation period is crucial, allowing the artist to shift attention away from the problem and trust that the mind will rest and the ideas will develop in due time.

Enlightenment

The elusive 'ah-ha' moment comes next. The deeper layers of the mind emerge and burst into conscious awareness after incubation. It happens when you are in the shower, walking, or occupied with something completely unrelated. It seems that the solution appears out of nowhere.

Verification

After the "aha" moment, the ideas and insights from phase 3 are further refined. The artist thinks carefully about their work and tells others how good it is. This involves translating ideas into written words, paint, or clay and developing a business plan.

What is expected from creative thinking?

There are many methods to apply innovative problem-solving in everyday situations, even if you believe you aren't creative.

Thinking creatively is not difficult; it just takes practice

Building your creative skills is critical to innovation.

Often, creative thinking involves tapping into different thinking styles and examining information from various perspectives to discover new patterns.

Examples of creative thinking

Creative thinking is valuable in various situations, not only in traditionally creative industries.

One way creative thinking is helpful is by identifying the right problem.

Using divergent thinking strategies can help you examine a situation from every angle and determine the actual root of the issue.

Once you've found the root problem, you can use lateral or convergent thinking to discover new solutions that may not have been apparent before.

Adding constraints, such as a timeline or budget to your project, can also help guide a creative thinking session.

For example, you might brainstorm how to manage a problem if your budget was cut in half. Constraints help spark unique ideas that you might have otherwise overlooked.

The importance of creative thinking

Falling into the same thinking patterns is common, especially at work. However, these patterns can limit your ability to innovate and keep you stuck in routines that no longer benefit you.

Creative thinking demostrates that there are multiple solutions to any problem, and honing this skill helps you identify innovative solutions more efficiently.

Moreover, creativity was the most in-demand soft skill in 2020, so developing your creative abilities can distinguish you in the workplace.

Creative thinking is vital for recognizing non-apparent patterns through deliberate thought and focus. Thinking creatively enhances your problem-solving skills, which has extensive benefits in both professional and personal activities.

Expressive and creative thinking allows us to challenge our assumptions, discover new aspects of ourselves and our perspectives, stay mentally sharp, and even become more optimistic.

1.6 Critical thinking

Thinking critically involves thinking clearly and rationally while recognizing the logical connection between concepts. It requires individuals to deduce the reasoning behind everything and be active learners rather than passive information receivers. A critical thinker will question ideas and assumptions, rather than accept them as they are. Good critical thinkers constantly strive to determine whether ideas, arguments, and findings represent the complete picture of a particular claim.

What is critical thinking?

Critical thinking is not simply about thinking outside the box but consistently and clearly understanding the rational connection between ideas.

It involves systematically discovering, analysing, and solving problems. Assertion and argument, assertion and assumption, assertion and conclusion, assertion and course of action, cause and effect, and similar elements are all key components of critical thinking. Now, let's look at the different types of critical thinking.

Stages of critical thinking

To reach a conclusion, ideas must go through several stages. We can summarise the main stages of critical thinking as follows:

- Identifying the problem or question: The narrower the problem, the easier it is to find solutions and answers.

- Gathering data and opinions: Find various sources presenting different ideas and perspectives.

- How reliable are the sources of information? Are their conclusions supported by data or just argumentative? Do we have enough evidence to support our ideas?

- Identifying assumptions: Are you sure the sources you've found are unbiased? Are you confident that you haven't been biased in your search for answers?

- Establishing the significance: What information is most important to you? Is the sample size sufficient? Are all opinions and arguments relevant to the problem you are attempting to solve?

- Making a decision and concluding: Identify the possible conclusions and decide which (if any) are sufficiently supported. All possible options should be weighed against their strengths and limitations.

Characteristics of critical thinking

Good critical thinking is a process that requires strong cognitive skills and positive mental attributes. It's important to use critical thinking skills like analyzing, evaluating, figuring out, inferring, and calculating.

These characteristics of this type of thinking are as follows:

- Curiosity is one of the most significant characteristics of critical thinking. Research shows that being curious makes us want to learn more and better ourselves so we can make good choices.

- Inquiry is a crucial critical thinking component, so it is important to be analytical. Analytical thinking involves the breakdown of intricate concepts into their simplest forms.

- Another characteristic of critical thinking is the ability to draw logical conclusions based on the review of available facts, events, and ideas. Analysing available information and observing patterns and trends will help you find connections and make informed decisions based on what will happen.

Examples of critical thinking

Here are some examples of critical thinking:

- You read a news story in the newspaper, but before sharing it, you try to verify the information by doing all possible research, including online sources.

- Some scholars who studied the most important theories behind the universe's formation realised that previous research had gaps. They then conducted additional experiments to find the truth.

- Always seek the truth when you provide information. For example, the notary costs 10k for everyone. You seek out notaries and ask for a quote.

Importance

Why is critical thinking important? The quality of your life depends on the decisions you make. If you want to ensure that you live your life in the best way possible, with tremendous success and happiness, you must make conscious choices.

Critical thinking is needed to achieve this. Critical thinking can help you understand yourself better, avoiding damaging or limiting beliefs and focusing on your strengths. Your quality of life can be improved by being able to express yourself.

Critical thinking is universal; regardless of your path or profession, these skills will always be relevant and valuable for success.

Critical thinking empowers us to solve problems and seek new and creative ideas. It also allows us to examine ideas and tailor them to ourselves and our situation.

We need this type of thinking because it helps us reflect on ourselves and find a basis for our opinions or ways of living, as well as tools for evaluation.

Understanding thoughts

Your thoughts play a significant role in your feelings and behaviors.

Many times, we aren't even aware of how we are thinking, and this can influence our reactions and emotions. So, the more you understand and recognise your thoughts, the more power you have to change your moods and behaviours.

Our thoughts come first and determine how we feel and how we respond. Hence, by altering one's thoughts, one can alter their impact on one's thinking and behavior. For example, if you send a message to a friend who doesn't respond immediately, you might think they are upset, making you feel nervous and stressed.

In the same situation, if they still need to check their phone, you're more likely to carry on with your day.

You can change your mood by bringing awareness to your thoughts. Once you have this awareness, you can start to change your thoughts. Always remember that thoughts are not facts until we act on them so we can change what we think.

Sometimes, our thoughts worsen things for us, and sometimes, our feelings can worsen things for us. So, if we have a strong feeling and think about something, it can affect how we think. Sometimes, if we think about something in a negative way, it can affect our feelings.

Recognizing and managing our thoughts and feelings is important for self-awareness and personal growth.

Additionally, the more aware you are of what is happening inside you and can distinguish between your thoughts and feelings, the easier it is to communicate them when needed. When you pay attention to yourself, you'll realize when you're combining a feeling and a thought.

Thus, the more we are self-aware and use the language of feelings to identify our emotions, the easier it will become.

By isolating your feelings, you can better understand your thoughts, even when experiencing a strong emotion like anger.

It will help you understand how your thoughts and feelings affect your life by expanding your emotional vocabulary and self-awareness. The more time you spend on self-awareness, the more control you will have in responding to situations rather than reacting to them.

In conclusion, we must learn to understand and manage our thoughts without being overwhelmed. If we lose balance, our perception of reality will become distorted, leading to stress, and adverse effects on our physical and mental health.

The subsequent chapters will provide a comprehensive examination of this condition and its potential impact on our daily lives.

Chapter 2
The sidewalk of excessive thoughts

Every thought originates from life, and when humans realised that thinking was necessary to achieve goals, even survival, they began to recognise and use it.

2.1 Why do we overthink?

Overthinking is a difficult habit to break. You might even convince yourself that overthinking something can help you develop the best solution, but usually, this is not the case. When you dwell on something for too long, your energy drains, and you cannot take appropriate and productive actions.

Moreover, constantly reflecting on worst-case scenarios, all the things you could have done, or anticipating your decisions while letting your mind wander can be exhausting.

Overthinking involves excessively analysing a particular topic or situation over extended periods. When you overthink, you struggle to focus on other issues and become consumed by the one thing you're fixated on.

Overthinking can be helpful because it involves looking at a problem from almost every possible angle and anticipating future events, according to some people. Studies show that thinking too much can lead to feelings of sadness, worry, and post-traumatic stress disorder.

Everyone sometimes overthinks, but finding ways to stop overthinking can be a liberating experience.

It can help you take action instead of merely dwelling on things that bother you. Rather than continuously replaying something in your mind, you can start taking the necessary steps to resolve the situation, bringing a sense of relief and empowerment.

An overthinker can easily confirm that the progression of overthinking stifles and exhausts you and that all of that thinking ends up being a complete waste of time by the end of the day.

Overthinking is regarded as unproductive and may result in rumination.

It hinders the enjoyment of daily activities and disrupts our emotional regulation and sleep habits.

It's a vicious cycle, known as an unhealthy routine, that leads to stress and causes the person to focus only on negative aspects and worries about future events while also dwelling on the past.

Excessive worry and stress can lead to symptoms of overthinking, such as irritability, fatigue, difficulty concentrating or remembering things, and insomnia. Digestive problems and tension in the shoulders and neck are also common physical symptoms associated with stress and anxiety.

If you're wondering whether you're overthinking a particular situation or concern, some specific signs indicate it. They include:

- The inability to think about anything else
- Being unable to relax
- Constantly feeling worried or anxious
- Fixating on things outside of your control
- Feeling mentally exhausted
- Having many negative thoughts
- Replaying a situation or experience in your mind
- Trying to anticipate your decisions
- Thinking about all the worst-case scenarios

2.2 The quantity of thoughts in our minds can be a problem, but even more so, the quality of these thoughts.

Some thoughts, like fantasies or anticipation of your weekend plans, may elicit feelings of pleasure and excitement.

However, negative thoughts can affect your mood and mind for a long time.

Worries about your relationship, work performance, or health: each of these can pop up and distract you from your activity and productivity.

Due to the negativity bias, we tend to attribute more significance to these negative thoughts, even if they do not represent an immediate or likely threat.

What you're worried about may not even happen, yet you still find it difficult to stop thinking and replaying the same thoughts over and over throughout the day.

Experts don't know how many negative thoughts people usually have, but it's clear that mental health problems like depression and anxiety can make it harder to stop thinking bad things. We should not forget that negative thoughts are one of the causes that lead to stress, depression, and anxiety, a vicious cycle.

It is possible for anxiety and depression to focus on a cycle of distressing or dark thoughts without exploring solutions.

It is important to remember that not all thoughts are negative; we may also have a significant number of positive thoughts, and that is good.

In conclusion, it is clear that the quality of our thoughts strongly influences our mental health.

If we get caught up in the spiral of negative thoughts, we are merely taking a step toward anxiety and depression. As we have said, with these two conditions, negative thoughts are triggered even more, leading us into a spiral of negativity.

2.3 Causes of overthinking

Why do people overthink?

We all do a lot of thinking, either to analyze or to reflect. Our time should be devoted to being thoughtful, critical, and curious about our thoughts. However, among us, some exceptional individuals desire to achieve better results! We are constantly told that "everything is better when done in moderation."

People who have crossed the line often don't realize they've crossed the line until it gets worse. Therefore, we keep asking what makes us overthink and what can prevent us from falling into the spiral.

An individual who engages in excessive thinking can readily demonstrate how the process of overthinking impedes and exhausts them, resulting in a complete waste of time at the conclusion of the day.

Overthinking is characterised as unproductive and can further lead to rumination. It makes it hard to enjoy daily activities and makes it hard to sleep and regulate our emotions.

It's a vicious cycle. Overthinking is an unhealthy routine that causes more stress, as one focuses solely on the negative aspects and worries about future events.

Current theories suggest that thoughts are formed when nerve cells in your brain, or neurons, signal other cells by releasing neurotransmitters. In an extremely short time, countless other neurons respond, triggering a chain of active neurons along pathways in your brain.

While neurons can send these signals at any time, the events around you often trigger this process, sparking thoughts about those events.

A 2015 study also suggested that two adjacent regions in the brain's left temporal lobe work together to build thoughts.

These regions use a system of variables similar to algebra to encode known and new information into comprehensible thoughts.

Regarding the content of your thoughts, your daily life often plays a key role. After all, you are more likely to think about things you experience regularly.

This reveals the strong connection between mental health issues and musing. It can seem inevitable when distressing thoughts and emotions persist. It's possible that you're focused on them because you don't know how to get rid of them.

Potential causes of overthinking

Excessive thinking is primarily driven by stress and anxiety. Overthinking is also often caused by low self-esteem and insecurity. For example, during the recent pandemic, social distancing caused stress and anxiety, which is a natural response to fear. We worried about our future and uncertainties regarding illnesses, deaths, and finances, which triggered overthinking.

These situations led us down the path of overthinking.

Parenting and beliefs

Children may experience anxiety at different times in their lives, and it is normal.

It is essential for parents to understand that children worry and get stressed just like adults but about various topics such as school and friends. Their sources of anxiety and stress change depending on their developmental stage.

Parents should be understanding and supportive, helping them find the positive side of situations, even in difficult times.

Unfortunately, there are times when parents can unintentionally provoke or fuel their child's anxiety. This can be due to how the parents were raised and educated.

Let's analyse the main parenting styles and the consequences they can have on a child's mind:

- Authoritarian parenting: The parent sets rigid rules, leaving the child little room to negotiate or make mistakes.
- Authoritative parenting: The parent communicates effectively with the child and enforces without punishment.
- Permissive parenting. The child is allowed to act freely without following strict rules, which are minimal and rarely enforced.
- Uninvolved parents: Children have absolute freedom and rarely communicate with their

parents on any topic, including behavioural rules, because such rules do not exist.

There is clear evidence that how a parent raises and educates a child can influence their growth and development. Adolescents and post-adolescents between 14 and 18 are the most affected. The effects are evident in their academic performance and how they set goals.

An inadequate parenting approach can result in separation anxiety in young children. A classic manifestation of this symptom is a child who cries when their parents leave. However, this behaviour is normal in young children but should decrease as they age four. If this clinginess persists beyond early childhood, the child's emotional state should be further investigated.

Authoritarian parenting can increase anxiety and depression as it is based on strict and austere attitudes toward the child.

Children raised by authoritarian parents are often worried about things that a typical child shouldn't be concerned with.

In contrast, children who receive emotional support from their parents better control their emotions; they know how to remain calm and aware.

Children are shielded from stress and sadness by authoritative and permissive parenting. Children raised with this approach develop tolerance and feel much less pressure.

Interestingly, childhood anxiety associated with parenting styles appears to be more pronounced in girls than in boys, but this phenomenon has yet to find a solid scientific basis.

A particularly alarming statistic concerns girls who feel abandoned or rejected by their parents; this sense of "rejection" often leads to such deep depression that some attempt suicide at least once in their lives.

In conclusion, professionals recommend monitoring children for any general disorders that an inappropriate parenting style might cause.

Given all the potential issues that can arise in a child or adolescent, many experts suggest educating children from an early age about the causes and symptoms of stress, anxiety, and depression so that they are aware of what they might face throughout their lives.

Desire to make the right decision

After all, examining a problem from every possible angle might make one believe they can reach a conclusion and solution more quickly. However, overthinking has the opposite effect: it creates barriers and complicates our ability and clarity in making decisions. When you overthink, you waste a lot of time seeking second opinions or exploring other options, which may be of little significance in the end, especially in minor matters. The pertinent inquiry is: What is the rationale behind individuals' obsession with certain objects? Overthinking sometimes leads you to reconsider decisions you've already made, causing you to waste a lot of time reflecting and getting upset over decisions you've taken, wishing you had chosen differently. Overthinking is a form of mental torment, while a bit of self-analysis can be truly helpful in avoiding repetitive behaviours. The fear of making the wrong choice haunts us when we're faced with a decision. This fear of failure isn't necessarily bad, but only if it inspires thoughts of success and motivates assertive actions towards a desired goal.

Where does the fear of not succeeding come from? The fear of making the wrong choice is often the reason for it, which is usually triggered by overthinking.

Handling problems responsibly

Throughout the day, we often have many questions that lead us to overthink. Rather than reducing uncertainty, overthinking traps us in a spiral of questions and doubts.

This not only leaves us in limbo, but it can also create new problems in our lives. Overthinking can't sleep and you're more likely to get a mental illness, according to studies.

The difference between overthinking and problem-solving is important. Sometimes, it's easy to confuse the two and convince ourselves that ruminating, obsessing, and worrying are somehow productive. Let's clarify this difference.

The solution to a problem does not necessarily come from thinking harder.

Our time and mental energy are the most valuable resources we have. Investing those resources in solving problems is wise rather than wasting time overthinking.

Problem-solving is the act of finding a solution. Simply put, you want to improve your skills, use plans, and take action. When you reduce stress, you'll know that you're solving problems. Overthinking involves a lot of thinking, worrying, and ruminating.

These actions make you focus on the problem and prevent you from coming up with a solution.

Thinking too much can make you feel upset and cause you to focus on negative thoughts. This can make you feel anxious all the time.

Be careful when you want to think about something too much. If you're solving problems, continue. If you need to be more analytical, refrain from wasting more time ruminating.

You can dedicate your resources to productive activity once you learn to solve problems rather than overthink. You will possess the mental fortitude to allocate your time and energy towards valuable pursuits that will assist you in achieving your full potential.

Stressful situations

Anxiety is a strong emotion that can affect our mental and physical health. When we feel anxious, we often focus on worst-case scenarios, which can lead to overthinking.

Overthinking means thinking about something for too long and getting tired of it. In response to anxiety, our bodies enter a fight-or-flight state, triggered by the release of stress hormones like adrenaline and cortisol. This physiological response prepares us to react to perceived threats.

However, heightened alertness causes our minds to constantly scan our environment for potential dangers, leading to overthinking and fixation on worst-case scenarios.

This type of thinking can be draining and make us feel trapped in our thoughts. It is essential to learn how to manage anxiety levels in order to overcome overthinking caused by anxiety and stress. It is possible to become more aware of our thoughts and feelings by practicing mindfulness meditation.

Mindfulness can also teach us to accept our thoughts without judging them, making negative thoughts less powerful. It can also help us learn to accept our thoughts without judgement.

In conclusion, anxiety and, consequently, stress play a significant role in overthinking. By learning to manage our anxiety levels, we can reduce the negative impact on our feelings and emotions.

We can learn to stop thinking too much and live a more peaceful and productive life. The key to changing your negative thoughts is to understand how you think now and the problems that come up.

Our thoughts, emotions, and behaviors are all connected, which means that our thoughts influence how we feel and act. Hence, notwithstanding the occasional occurrence of unfavorable thoughts, it is imperative to be cognizant of the appropriate course of action to prevent their impact on the course of our day.

Chapter 3
Characteristics of overthinking

In the previous chapter, we discussed overthinking and its potential causes. Now, let's understand how to recognise the signs of overthinking in ourselves or others.

Excessive worry and stress can lead to symptoms like irritability, fatigue, difficulty concentrating, memory problems, and insomnia. Physical symptoms such as digestive issues and tension in the shoulders and neck are also associated with stress and anxiety. So, it's important to know when you're thinking too much and take action to fix it.

3.1 They begin to relate their decisions to their fears

Overthinking decisions can prevent you from taking action. When faced with a multitude of options and unable to make a decision between A and B, it is common to opt for C or succumb to paralysis, procrastination, or the inability to make a decision at all. Let's consider a practical example of what decision-making might look like for someone who overthinks:

Once upon a time, a woman named Lara struggled to make decisions. She was a perfectionist, always worried about making the wrong choice.

Whether it was choosing what to wear, what to watch, or where to eat, she spent hours, if not days, weighing the pros and cons of each option before finally making a decision.

This tendency to overthink became a real problem for Lara.

Decision paralysis was causing her to miss out on various opportunities. She couldn't commit to a career, a relationship, or even a simple outing with friends because she couldn't decide what to do.

Her friends and family grew frustrated because they never knew if she would show up for events or follow through on plans. She became anxious and depressed, and her relationships suffered as a result.

One day, Lara had to choose between two job offers. One was at a large company with a higher salary but more extended hours and stress. There was a smaller start-up with a lower paycheck but a better work-life balance.

She was so paralysed by the fear of making the wrong choice that she did nothing.

Lara's story exemplifies decision paralysis and how our decisions can turn into fears and inaction.

Decision paralysis occurs when you become overwhelmed by a decision, whether it's complicated or simple. It can cause you to overthink, delay the decision, or avoid it altogether.

There are 3 main reasons for decision paralysis:

- It's more complicated than ever to make decisions in this hyper-developed world because there are so many options.

- Making a choice involves risk, including disappointment, fear or regret. Our inability to regulate the emotional aspect of decision-making affects our ability to choose between options.

- Your brain struggles to make sense of important, complex, and abstract tasks. This is called executive function, which refers to how your brain manages decision-making and prioritises what's important.

3.2 They Usually Need Approval from Others

People who overthink may soon become insecure, constantly seeking approval from others to make decisions or take any action. It's easy to provoke worries; think about it whenever you question what others might think of you. In this case, you're almost certainly creating discomfort in your mind, which leads to stress, insecurity, and anxiety. People who respond slowly to an email aren't necessarily avoiding you. They may still need to read it or be busy with other projects.

Worrying about someone's honest opinion is worse than obsessing about something that doesn't exist.

We often seek validation from others because we think we can't handle rejection or unrecognition. If you blame yourself when people don't approve of your choices or aren't supportive, you may need to lower your self-criticism and increase your self-compassion.

For example, if your boss isn't pleased with a decision you made or a task you completed differently from how they would have done it, remember that everyone can make mistakes, or rather, they may have different ways of doing things. You can't please everyone, but your self-worth shouldn't depend on that.

In conclusion, just because someone else thinks something about you doesn't mean it's a fact.

Not only do those who grant their approval have power over you, but you're also digging your path to insecurity.

Building your self-esteem from the inside out and strengthening your authentic self will serve you much better than a substitute sense of self.

It is healthy to seek confirmation and reassurance from time to time. It takes courage to ask for support when we need it, and we all have moments when we question ourselves. It is not healthy to constantly need reassurance. When it becomes a routine mechanism for anxiety, it can lead to a self-perpetuating cycle that can be hard to break.

3.3 They are prone to pessimism

As we've seen before, overthinking often leads to pessimism.

The mother's story at the beginning of our journey showed how overthinkers tend to blow events out of proportion, leading to overwhelming feelings.

Their mental health is affected by this, as well as their physical health.

Maintaining realistic expectations and avoiding extreme positive or negative perspectives is key to good health and happiness. Research suggests that having low levels of pessimism, rather than high levels of optimism, is linked to better health.

Pessimism, on the other hand, can contribute to cardiovascular disease and other bodily and psychological health issues, while optimism isn't always a defense mechanism. Instead of constantly striving for an overly positive or negative attitude, the goal is to have a balanced optimism with a touch of pessimism each day.

3.4 They Create Imaginary Scenarios in Their Mind

As previously mentioned, overthinkers often harbour negative thoughts and tend to catastrophise situations.

Catastrophising is a cognitive distortion where the mind distorts information into an imaginary worst-case scenario.

Knowing the issue can make it overwhelming and difficult for people to recognize it.

We all daydream at some point in our lives, and it's not always a positive thing but could be caused by adverse events we have gone through that we cannot overcome or because of mental health problems such as anxiety or long-term sadness.

These daydreams often involve unreal scenarios rather than real memories; hence, they are false scenarios.

Instead of considering positive outcomes, individuals create scenarios based solely on potential negative consequences, leading to chaotic and exhausting thoughts.

Although it's natural for the mind to wander, daydreaming about negative events can lead to increased worry and harm mental health, often resulting in the creation of false and damaging scenarios.

While occasional thoughts and worries are normal, if they start interfering with everyday life, this pattern of harmful thinking becomes a problem.

Quality of life and fear-based thinking can be negatively impacted.

This kind of thinking, known as catastrophic thinking, can be associated with mental health issues and illnesses.

It's not an official medical condition but often indicates various disorders such as anxiety, depression, and post-traumatic stress disorder.

3.5 They believe the rest of the world is angry with them.

Overthinkers often have the impression that others are upset with them.

Instead of trying to manage everyone's emotions, reminding ourselves of our responsibilities would be helpful.

You're responsible for managing your anxiety, while others are responsible for managing theirs, communicating their thoughts, and expressing if they're upset.

When we worry, automatic thoughts come into play. Some may be realistic, while others are distortions of reality.

Our minds make us think we understand what someone else is thinking. For example, a friend makes a particular facial expression, and we're convinced they're angry with us.

The more you read into someone's mind and believe what you're thinking, the more your brain will engage in mind-reading. Your brain assumes you find it helpful, so it keeps doing it.

In this mindset, you're constantly worried about how others perceive you, affecting how you behave and see yourself. Remember that they're likely not talking or even thinking about you, but your mind can play tricks on you and convince you they are.

For all the reasons mentioned above, it makes no sense to keep thinking that others are angry with us because, in most cases, it's just our imagination.

3.6 They tend to be quite emotional.

As discussed in this chapter, several cognitive distortions can influence our thinking. Emotional reasoning is one of the most prevalent. An individual assumes that something must be true because they feel something.

We all experience this to some extent from time to time. For example, it's part of our tendency to believe things that support our biases, often without much concrete evidence.

Emotional reasoning can lead to many problems. This can be seen through the prism of cognitive-behavioral therapy.

This type of reasoning assumes that because you're experiencing a negative emotion, it must accurately reflect reality; it's a way of self-judging based solely on your feelings.

Emotional reasoning occurs when your feelings are so powerful that you believe they point to a certain objective truth. There are no conditions or the need for facts or evidence that you feel are true. Negative emotions and mental states are associated with this. Teenagers who feel stupid and ugly might conclude that they are unintelligent and unattractive.

Your emotions can significantly impact your thoughts, behaviours, and reasoning. Emotional reasoning can arise from various situations, many of which are traumatic or involve some form of danger (real or perceived).

Consider the example of Lara, a 20-year-old woman driving home from work one evening when a violent storm suddenly hits.

While seeking shelter, Lara ends up in a puddle and has an accident. Despite being physically unharmed and the car only sustaining minor damage, Lara refuses to drive in the rain from then on, convinced that she will have another accident.

If you feel guilty, emotional reasoning may lead you to conclude that you are a terrible person.

Research indicates that this distortion is common among individuals who suffer from anxiety and depression, and it is a prevalent thought pattern among many people.

Different types of therapy can assist in recognising and addressing the signs of emotional reasoning.

Remember that just because we're scared doesn't mean there's a real threat.

Our minds often create or seek out situations that align with our internal experiences, resulting in the fabrication of problems that don't exist.

Emotional reasoning is frequently associated with panic disorders.

Negative self-talk that heightens emotions can lead to a severe panic attack for people struggling with emotional reasoning.

3.7 They tend to worry excessively about the people around them.

One common cognitive distortion of overthinkers is focusing excessively on the thoughts and reactions of others while neglecting their thoughts and emotions. They tend to place more importance on how others handle situations.

When we overthink, we analyse various problems and scenarios, as well as potential options and outcomes. Additionally, overthinkers spend a lot of time contemplating how the people around them might react. This results in prioritising others' feelings over their own and minimising their emotions.

It often happens that, overthinkers frequently set aside their own problems to focus on solving others' issues, becoming mere spectators in others' lives and adding extra burdens to their own thoughts.

3.8 They are prone to turning their condition into an addiction.

People who overthink often engage in brooding.

Negative feelings and distress and their causes and consequences are repeatedly thought about. Overthinking can lead to a focus on past events, triggering memories of similar situations and creating a gap between one's authentic self and ideal self. This can cause guilt and a feeling of not doing things differently in a given circumstance.

Due to its repetitive and harmful nature, brooding can contribute to depression or anxiety.

When a depressed person contemplates, they are more likely to remember negative things that have happened to them in the past, interpret their current life situations negatively, and feel hopeless about the future.

Furthermore, brooding can hinder problem-solving and make it difficult to move forward. Overthinking can contribute to negative emotions in individuals without depression or anxiety.

It's tough to break free from these thoughts because this cycle can make you feel worse, think more, and develop an addiction to them.

Since we have written this book to help you avoid overthinking, let's outline its consequences so you can reflect on your current situation and possibly diagnose your overthinking tendencies.

Once we find it, we'll give you some advice on how to fix it.

3.9 What are the consequences of overthinking?

How do I know if I am overthinking?

We have analysed the problem of overthinking step by step. We started by understanding what thinking is, where it originates, the types of thoughts, what overthinking is, and its main characteristics.

Let's try to understand the main signs that identify us as overthinkers.

Everyone occasionally overthinks things, but the truth is that everyone does.

It's true, however, that thinking too much can affect your mental well-being. Mental health declines make it increasingly tempting to overthink. It's a vicious downward spiral, really.

Nonetheless, it can be challenging to discern during a storm. It is advantageous to contemplate and contemplate about matters. What is the purpose of seeking a superior resolution without contemplating it? To avoid repeating the mistake, you must keep thinking about it.

There exist several warning signs that indicate excessive thinking, including:

- I am unable to refrain from worrying.
- I frequently experience anxiety regarding matters that are beyond my control.
- I consistently remind myself of my errors.
- I replay embarrassing moments over and over again.
- I never shut off my brain.
- When I recollect conversations with individuals, I cannot help but reflect on the things I regret having said or not said.

- I devote a significant amount of my free time to contemplating the concealed significance of individuals' words and events.

- I often dwell on choices made or phrases said by people close to me that don't align with what I would have done or said.

- I often miss what is happening in the present because I spend so much time worrying about the future.

Your mind doesn't stop

Is it like your mind never stops working? Are you having trouble unwinding because you're constantly thinking and worrying?

You're not alone if you've ever laid in bed wondering, "Why can't I fall asleep?"

There are many reasons for a frantic or busy mind.

You can find the best ways to calm your mind by understanding why you can't turn it off.

Stress is a usual suspect when you can't stop thinking.

Stress causes your body to release cortisol, which helps you stay alert. This means that your brain also stays alert, even when you don't want it to.

You can't relax or sleep because cortisol can make you feel anxious.

It's possible to keep thinking the same things over and over again without ever finding a way to fix the issue or worry.

It can feel like your brain has been hijacked. Even when you realize you're overthinking, recognise that it's unproductive, and try to push the thoughts away. They won't stop.

The thoughts seem to take on a life of their own.

You suffer from insomnia

Sometimes, our worries can have a real impact. We can't sleep, and we overthink every little thing.

People who live with stress, anxiety, depression, and insomnia often say that unwanted intrusive thoughts make it harder for them to fall asleep than any physical discomfort or pain.

Insomnia and overthinking usually go hand in hand.

So, people with insomnia commonly try to block out thoughts that keep them from sleeping, which might seem sensible but, in the long run, does more harm than good.

By implementing more effective strategies to address intrusive thoughts, the interval between bedtime and slumber can be made less challenging.

You might also find it easier to fall back asleep if your sleep isn't interrupted by intrusive and frantic thoughts.

Numerous thought-blocking strategies have been studied for dealing with these intrusive thoughts in the context of insomnia.

The core of these strategies is allowing people to replace thoughts that might keep them awake (stimulating thoughts) with non-stimulating thoughts. This should:

- reduce the time it takes to fall asleep (sleep onset time)
- help you stop overthinking

- Increase sleep quality.

Some situations aren't easily forgotten.

For some, memories fade over time, but not for everyone. Those who suffer from anxiety conditions tend to enter a loop that makes them relive the past or specific moments of their life repeatedly. When this happens, a strong sense of unease and discomfort arise in these individuals.

As the name suggests, short-term memories last briefly, while some are transferred to long-term memory. Images and sounds can prompt the brain to recall a long-term memory, even if we prefer not to.

While we tend to forget trivial information, our brains are more likely to store significant details.

Due to the involvement of a specific area of the brain, emotional memories are difficult to forget. Thanks to a part of our brain called the amygdala, our thoughts are reprocessed and recoded, making them more memorable.

Memories tend to be more memorable when accompanied by intense emotions. Research suggests that the more intense the memory, the more vivid the resulting recollection of that event. However, as we're analysing, memories only sometimes help us. Remembering feelings of terror can help us face a particular situation and keep us out of danger. Still, it can become an obstacle when these thoughts are perpetual and prevent us from living peacefully every day. Since it's not always easy to let go of old habits, it may be helpful, even for our personal growth, to learn new methods to manage unpleasant memories, feeling less overwhelmed by their weight when they resurface.

The brain holds onto embarrassing moments

As mentioned, events that trigger strong emotional reactions are usually more memorable. Emotions can be positive or negative, but bad things tend to stick out more clearly in our memories.

This is why it's easy to recall moments that made us feel embarrassed or rejected. However, even though a memory looks pretty vivid, it may not be accurate.

The same research indicates that when adverse events occur, we tend to focus on the worst parts and give them more attention than necessary.

Of course, it's not helpful to pretend something didn't happen if it did, but acknowledging that our brains may not always show a balanced picture can help reduce our distress.

Feeling embarrassed or ashamed when intrusive memories resurface is normal. However, it's vital not to let these feelings trap you in the past.

You can avoid situations or people that remind you of embarrassing moments if you have persistent thoughts of embarrassing moments.

We worry that others will think less of us if they find out about our past mistakes or embarrassing moments, leading to a lot of embarrassment. As a result, we may try to suppress these memories, but this approach can backfire.

Attempting to avoid thinking about something often makes the memory more likely to resurface. Instead of trying to forget an embarrassing memory, accepting it and finding humour in it might be more helpful. Sharing the event with someone close to us who won't judge us can also help us see the lighter side of the situation.

It is imperative to bear in mind that every individual experiences embarrassing moments and commits errors. This fact can help us overcome our embarrassment and move forward. Whether we choose to accept or laugh at our embarrassing memories, it's crucial to remember that everyone has faced similar experiences at some point. Managing and letting go of embarrassing memories is an important step toward maturity and good mental health, and seeking help to overcome specific memories should not be a source of embarrassment. With patience and time, we can learn to let go of the past and move forward towards a brighter future.

Too much doubt

A moderate level of self-criticism can motivate us to work harder and improve our skills, thus boosting our confidence. However, excessive self-doubt and fear can hinder us from reaching our full potential. Insecurity, which is a lack of confidence in oneself and one's abilities, can hold us back from success and believing in ourselves. While humility is a healthy trait, it can become detrimental if it results in self-sabotage. As William Shakespeare once stated, "Our doubts are traitors, and they can lead us to lose the good we may have gained by frightening to attempt," indicating that doubt can prevent us from attempting.

Although learning how to overcome doubts is essential, understanding their causes can also be helpful. Insecurity can be caused by several factors. Being too hard on ourselves can be helped by identifying the sources of doubt. Overcoming doubts is usually more critical than pinpointing their exact causes. The fear of failure and the pressure of not disappointing others are among the primary motivators behind self-doubt. An overthinker may come to believe that luck, rather than their talents, got them this far.

Doubts in an overthinker also manifest as indecision or difficulty making big and small decisions because they worry that whatever they choose will be wrong.

Let's start taking back control of our lives, enjoying the moments and pushing excessive thoughts out of our minds.

Through this chapter, you've likely had the chance to understand whether you, too, are an overthinker, have been one, or if some of these symptoms have occasionally presented themselves.

Well, don't worry; now we'll see how to banish overthinking from our lives once and for all with a series of practical exercises that will help us achieve our goal: a mind full of quality thoughts.

Chapter 4
Escaping the cage of excessive thoughts

Many people think that ignoring thoughts is the best approach, but this is probably the last method you should try.

Ignoring means you're putting a lot of energy into avoiding negative thoughts, so those thoughts are still in your head, even if you're trying to ignore them.

Acknowledging your negative thoughts and then working on processing them is most effective. There are steps you can take to change your ways of thinking once you recognize cognitive distortions.

Getting help is essential because these distorted thinking patterns can severely affect mental health and overall well-being.

Moving forward, we will explore different solutions to combat negative thoughts, manage anxiety, and enhance your quality of life.

What are the first steps to stop overthinking?

Human nature is fundamentally concerned with worrying and torturing oneself with thoughts. When it spirals out of control, it can have negative impacts on health and increase the risk of certain mental and physical disorders.

So, what should someone who overthinks do? Let's explore some ideas and suggestions for taking the first steps toward a better state.

4.1 Recognise patterns

If you tend to overthink, you know the feeling all too well. It's like a problem keeps replaying in your mind, whether it's a health worry or a work issue, and you can't stop fixating on it, desperately searching for a solution or meaning.

The thoughts keep going in circles, and unfortunately, the solutions rarely come.

If we spend too much time thinking about our problems and choices, we often feel more confused than when we started. What's more, persistent overthinking can lead to a range of symptoms, such as insomnia, difficulty concentrating, and lack of energy. And then, we start worrying about these symptoms, creating a vicious cycle of excessive thoughts. In some cases, this can eventually lead to chronic anxiety or depression.

When overthinking becomes too much to handle and the associated symptoms become overwhelming, it's only natural to look for ways to calm down. Many common strategies might seem like they would help, but research shows that they can actually cause more harm than good, leading to even more overthinking.

People often focus on the past and worry too much about the future when they have negative thoughts. This tends to trap you in a cycle of excessive and negative thoughts, which can accompany or even worsen anxiety and other disorders. Meditation and distraction can help interrupt this cycle.

Ruminating is common to many health conditions and has close links to past negative experiences.

It can feel like a loop you can't get out of.

What does it mean to ruminate?

The American Psychological Association (APA) defines rumination as " obsessive thinking that involves excessive and repetitive thoughts or themes, which can interfere with other forms of mental activity". This can result in numerous health and mental issues.

In addition to being a symptom, the habit of ruminating can affect a person's health by:

- prolonging or intensifying depression
- impairing the ability to think and process emotions
- causing or worsening anxiety, sleep problems, and impulsive behaviours
- exacerbating and sustaining stress responses, leading to chronic stress
- increasing the risk of inflammation and physical health problems due to stress
- increase the risk of substance use disorders

The act of ruminating can transform worry into a routine or a way of life.

In 2005, the APA listed some common reasons for rumination, such as:

- the belief that ruminating will provide insights into your life or a problem
- have a history of emotional or physical trauma
- dealing with ongoing stressors that you cannot control

If you ruminate, you may be more likely to:

- focus on adverse past events and blame yourself.
- interpret current events more negatively
- feel hopeless about the future

Rumination can be a complex cycle to break, but there are ways to stop these intrusive thoughts. Promptly stopping such thoughts when they start can prevent them from intensifying.

Besides dwelling on the past, we are often worried about the future.

As we've discussed in previous chapters, these two actions (ruminating and worrying about the future) are often connected and are clear signs of an overthinking mind.

Inquiring about the future is a common occurrence and, to a certain extent, beneficial; it enables us to plan and prepare for the future.

It's only when worry shifts from being "realistic and constructive" to "abnormal or unhealthy" that you might need to take action.

It can be problematic if your worry is exaggerated or what we call 'catastrophising' or if it's entirely out of perspective and impacts your ability to act.

Don't worry; various methods can help you manage your worries and gain a better perspective.

Research suggests that trying to suppress thoughts can make things worse, leading to what we call the "rebound effect."

The more someone tries to avoid worrying thoughts, the more persistent they become.

A more effective approach is to accept anxiety and worrisome thoughts or "let them be" and then work on finding solutions.

For example, if you're worried and stressed about certain things, acknowledge those worries and accept that they are honest and common problems.

Notice if situations become repetitive

The tendency to repeat past actions often involves re-creating painful situations that occurred in the past, re-enacting trauma, and unconsciously recreating the trauma.

Any experience where you feel overwhelmed by despair or fear is considered a trauma. You may feel compelled to relive these moments, even though they were painful and harmful to your well-being. However, this compulsion doesn't help you overcome the trauma and might worsen the situation.

Learning about the tendency to repeat can help you understand how to overcome it.

You may not be fully aware that you're engaging in this behaviour, so understanding the causes and symptoms can help prevent it from happening again (if you are indeed doing it).

You can live a healthier life once you know what you're dealing with.

Let's consider a practical example: You left your previous job because it was too stressful and demanding, and you became anxious every time you had to deliver a project.

So, you decided to start freelancing, where you manage your work schedule instead of having a boss.

However, whenever you have to deliver a project now, even as a freelancer, all those anxieties and fears from the past resurface, and you relive the trauma as if nothing has changed.

4.2 Identifying the cause of discomfort

In addition to recognising what you can control and cannot, it's essential to understand that our need for control is often rooted in our inability to tolerate discomfort. If we overthink something, we are trying to find answers to make ourselves feel better. Uncertainty is the greatest enemy of the human brain, and anxiety will almost always arise in situations where we don't know the outcomes.

Our ancestors needed certainty to survive, and therefore, uncertainty brought discomfort. Anxiety, associated with uncertainty, is a response designed to push us to find solutions. However, this does not mean seeking certainty is always the right approach.

As mentioned earlier, these answers won't always be found, so we either continue to think like a hamster on a wheel or learn to sit with discomfort.

If we become comfortable with not knowing the answers, we won't feel the need to search for them incessantly. The only way to relieve anxiety is to learn how to deal with it.

Accepting our anxiety is easier said than done, but self-regulation is something you can develop.

Mindfulness practices, meditation, and breathing exercises are all excellent ways to cultivate self-regulation. Calming the nervous system during stressful moments is a valuable tool to develop.

You need to develop tools to help you cope with your anxiety when it arises without overthinking to try and alleviate your discomfort.

It's hard to accept feeling uncomfortable, but it's important if you want to improve yourself. First, it is essential to recognize what makes you uncomfortable and understand how these situations make you feel; this will allow you to identify and conquer the conditions that trigger your discomfort. For growth, it is crucial to focus on all the factors that trigger your discomfort and confront them without delay. Discomfort often signals a need to stop what you're doing. Just like physical pain makes you stop exercising, emotional pain causes you to withdraw from specific experiences. Discomfort is often seen as a negative sign for personal growth.

4.3 Identifying our responsibilities

One important thing to understand is that many of the decisions we make, which may lead us to overthink, are our own.

Improving our mental health may not be easy, and in some cases, external professional help may be necessary, but the desire to change must always start from within.

If the work environment or job is the leading cause of your stress, consider changing jobs.

In order to accomplish this, it is imperative that you take matters into your own hands and resign. This also applies to being in a toxic romantic relationship or a friendship that doesn't make you feel good.

However, if you don't take action if the initiative doesn't come from you, then it will be your fault if you spend most of your time in the office, come home distressed, and constantly think about work.

Various external factors significantly influence our decisions, but ultimately, it is our responsibility to address our anxiety.

4.4 Gathering the information from the previous points

There are a wide range of symptoms that can be caused by persistent overthinking. These symptoms include insomnia, difficulty concentrating, and a decrease in energy, which frequently prompts additional concerns regarding these symptoms, resulting in a vicious cycle of overthinking. This, in turn, increases stress, depression, and anxiety, which in turn increases depression. Threat monitoring, seeking answers and reassurance, and over-planning are common strategies for controlling anxiety and worry, but they are counterproductive and often backfire. They usually lead to an increased sense of danger and more worries, reinforcing the belief that worry is beyond your control.

Many consider overthinking an innate personality trait that cannot be changed. However, overthinking, in terms of worry and rumination, is a learned strategy that we choose, consciously or unconsciously, to cope with our thoughts and feelings.

Overthinking is a habit we fall into, but we can learn to change it. It starts with a "trigger thought." It's not the trigger thought itself or the number of trigger thoughts that causes unpleasant symptoms.

It's how much time you spend engaging with these thoughts, ruminating, and worrying. While your trigger thoughts are entirely automatic, you can learn to control them.

Thoughts are fleeting and will pass if you don't invest energy in them, so it's a matter of deciding what to do: respond to them or let them run their course?

One way to challenge the belief that overthinking is beyond your control is to explore whether you can postpone your worries and ruminations.

Half an hour a day is a good time to worry and ruminate freely. When trigger thoughts arise earlier in the day, let go of the idea, like an itchy mosquito bite, and postpone engaging with it until the scheduled time. It's counterproductive to avoid situations that may provoke overthinking; you must learn to let them go and deal with them at the right moment.

Reprogramming the way we think about ourselves

Are you living the life you have always wanted, or are you just settling down? Have you reached your highest aspirations, or do you feel stuck, knowing you still need to achieve your full potential?

Are you living the life you've always wanted, or are you just settling? Have you reached your highest aspirations, or do you feel stuck, knowing you still need to achieve your full potential? To design a life that brings you fulfilment, joy, and passion, you can reprogram your mind to give you the focus and determination required.

Almost everyone knows what they can expect and deserve from life, but when life veers off the path we have quietly set, we often become frustrated and upset. "Why is this happening?" we ask ourselves. This discontent can be powerful; it can drive us to change.

But our subconscious can also work against us. Many of us turn our frustration and upset inward, sabotaging potential success.

We believe that we deserve better and might work harder for a while. But, instead of striving for lasting change, we fall back into our careers, finances, relationships, and health.

What if you were able to take control and learn to reprogram your mind? You could make your life a masterpiece by redirecting your focus.

Success hinges on your subconscious mind, and you have the power to change it. The time is right to take back control of your thoughts. If you are clear on what you deserve and want to achieve your goals, you can only act because our life is not made up of "what ifs" or "could haves." Our life is the sum of the actions we take.

The power of the mind is undeniable. Cultivating complete certainty and deep confidence in yourself requires understanding how to harness the subconscious mind's programming.

Our subconscious mind makes decisions without active thought. The subconscious mind is different from the conscious mind, which includes the thoughts we know we're having at any given moment. The unconscious mind holds past events and experiences that we don't remember.

The subconscious mind works well when learning to play an instrument. At first, you need to think about translating the sheet music and moving your fingers to play each note, but as you practice, you will be able to pick up any song and play it effortlessly.

Learning new skills is not the only thing the subconscious mind learns. It takes in information and shapes what we think, say, and do. Our beliefs and values are stored in the brain, which decides what to send to the conscious mind and what to save for later.

How long does it take to rewire your mind? It's possible to wait a month, a few weeks, or even longer.

The answer will be determined by how deeply ingrained the behavior you wish to alter is and your preconceptions regarding limitations.

In order to learn how to reprogram your mind for success, you must take three steps to change your mindset and direct your focus in the right direction.

- DECIDE - The first step is to have absolute clarity about what you want. Learn how to stop thinking about things and focus on your goals. What would you like to happen? The more you think about it, the more detail you show, and the stronger your vision will be. This creates a subconscious mental map, giving your brain the tools to turn that vision into reality.

Do you want to reprogram your subconscious? Consider a discussion with your life partner. When we are engaged in a heated exchange with a loved one, we often lose sight of the disagreement and focus on being heard, getting the last word, and winning.

You stop watching your tone and being kind to your partner and start treating them like adversaries. This is a quick way to escalate the argument and turn it into something worse.

Instead, stop and ask yourself why you are arguing. You are not engaged in combat for victory; rather, you are in disagreement regarding a matter and seek a resolution.

When you get distracted by the desire to win, you lose sight of the real issue. Your brain will be reprogrammed to use its resources to produce that result at that moment if you remember this.

Subconscious reprogramming begins with deciding what you want - now and in the future - and focusing on it gives your brain direction.

You should decide that you are not willing to settle and are eager to live as you are now. Start reprogramming your brain and set your sights on what you want.

- COMMIT - After deciding what you want, the next step in subconscious reprogramming is commitment. Free your mind from fear and self-doubt. How do you do that? By committing and letting yourself be guided.

Fear is one of the most challenging blocks to overcome and often inhibits people's ability to take action. Fears include rejection, failure, accomplishment, suffering, or the unknown.

If you do nothing, that fear will stay precisely where it is, blocking your path. You won't move, and you'll always live in fear, with that fear lingering in the back of your mind, keeping you from your goals. The lack of action allows negative thoughts to flourish: "It's a good thing I didn't try." I wouldn't have made it without you.

When you allow fear to seep into your subconscious, that negativity based on fear will permeate everything you think about yourself and everything you do.

The only way to face fear is to reprogram your mind by confronting it head-on.

You'll know what doesn't work if you try something and fail, and next time, you'll be better prepared and educated.

Reprogramming your brain means debunking negative rumours like the infamous "I can't".

Starting small and doing it every day will make it easier and maybe even exhausting at first. It will become a habit in no time.

Be true to yourself. Commit to overcoming negative thoughts and committing to a better life. The real power of subconscious mind programming is harnessed when you fully commit yourself, push to the next level, and demand more of yourself than anyone else could expect.

- RESOLVE - You should take an inventory of your situation once you have decided on the path you want to take. Resolution involves finding solutions to whatever challenges may arise.

A fundamental part of finding resolution is effectively reprogramming your brain.

Tunnel vision limits you: you may miss opportunities and alternative paths that could bring incredible benefits. Remember, you never have 100% control. Think about it: has your life gone exactly as planned? Probably not.

There is no straight line on the path you take. That's why it's essential to stay flexible: learn from mistakes, embrace failure, and use negativity to drive change. As long as you're making progress, you're on the right track as you're on the right track.

When you reprogram your mind to focus on resolution, you can change your approach to problems as needed.

Not all obstacles and circumstances are the same; true power comes from within, and reprogramming your brain conditions you for success.

Frustration becomes a gift because it means you're on the verge of a breakthrough. Failing is a learning experience, helping you improve in the future.

Any block you encounter becomes an opportunity for you to redirect and find a new, creative solution. This is what your brain can do to get things done.

Your future will always be determined by the way you think. If you want to improve your life and change your life, you must change your thinking. Hundreds of people worldwide are dissatisfied with their lives because of how they think. If you also feel this sense of frustration, then try moving forward with this book.

We must distance ourselves from and eliminate negative thoughts, especially those related to our personality.

To reprogram ourselves and our mental habits, we must start thinking that we can do everything we desire and aspire to have a better life that meets our expectations.

4.5 Redefining yourself every day

Believing in yourself is a powerful way to change your mindset. Tell yourself you're capable and capable of achieving your objectives. This belief is essential for your future success. For instance, if you are nervous about public speaking, remind yourself that it can be enjoyable and that you have the strength and ability to do it. To adopt a new mindset and create positive change, there are 5 key ways of thinking and acting that you should embrace. Planning is crucial for designing a positive change, as it helps you identify your goals and how to accomplish them. Here's how to change:

- Be curious. Reconnect with your childlike imagination and ask questions to discover new opportunities.
- Try things. As mentioned earlier, you can't just plan for the future. You need to make it happen.

Action is more important than just thinking. Remember this rule: 80% action, 20% thinking.

- Re-frame the issues. Find better solutions by looking at challenges from a different perspective.

- Understand that it's a process. Some ideas will be successful, while others won't. Mistakes are normal. Obstacles are natural. Embrace the ups and downs of the journey and focus on learning and growing from the experience.

- Ask for help. Collaboration and asking for help from others can be helpful in the design process.

For example, keeping a journal to track effective strategies for dealing with overthinking can be beneficial.

It's a simple yet powerful technique that allows you to reflect on your thoughts and feelings and gain valuable insights.

Journaling allows you to reflect on your thoughts and emotions, which can help you identify thought patterns and behaviors that contribute to overthinking.

4.6 Create a positive mantra

One of the best ways to overcome the effects of overthinking is by changing your mindset.

Using a positive mantra can shift your focus to something uplifting and stop worrying.

Negative thoughts often come from fear or insecurity, so changing your mantra to something positive can help get your mind back on track. When you can't find your way back, use a mantra that makes you feel better to distract your mind. Saying "everything's going to be alright" can be effective. Feelings of stress, fear and depression can be helped by mantras. If you're plagued by overthinking, positive affirmations are a great way to combat the habit. Positive affirmations can be written in a journal or spoken aloud to reinforce the positive aspects of your life. This practice can help you overcome daily challenges and bring you closer to what you truly want. Positive affirmations are helpful in many ways, including boosting confidence and self-esteem. They can also help you overcome difficult past experiences. You can live more fully in the moment by challenging your negative thoughts with affirmations. They're great for getting to sleep. It often takes a few weeks to become comfortable with the process.

If you want to make the process easier, try picturing positive affirmations. When you imagine them, you can feel calm and relaxed. You can write positive thoughts on cards or sticky notes and put them where people can see them. Affirmations can also be spoken aloud to others. Overthinking is an unhealthy habit. It can affect your mind and well-being and is difficult to break. Overthinking isn't just bad for your mind, it's also bad for you. You can live without worries and anxiety by implementing positive affirmations. Try to recognise a phrase that resonates with you and see its impact on your body. You can choose to say your mantra whenever you prefer or when you have time, but it has been proven that doing so in the morning, right after you wake up, is more effective. Try to imprint the mantra or mantras that make you feel better into your mind and use them whenever you feel overwhelmed by negative thoughts to return to positive thinking. Below are some mantras that might be useful, but remember, anything that soothes you is fine! There are no standards.

Here are the mantras:

- I let go of all my thoughts connected to the past because I cannot change what happened.
- I feel peace in my mind.
- I am seeing things differently.

It is important to change the mantras every few days.

You can create inviting mantras to target specific areas or use one for an extended period. If a mantra no longer has a calming effect, then it's time to revise it. When these mantras become integral to your existence, you can truly benefit from them. Refer to your mantras to help you stop over-focusing because, as we've already mentioned, overthinkers get caught up in their thoughts. By diverting your thoughts with a mantra, you can finally be free from overthinking.

4.7 Being present in the moment

What could be worse than worrying about the future? When you start to worry about the fact that you are worried.

The good news is that mindfulness or being present in the moment can help break this cycle.

Practising mindful meditation, even for a few minutes, can keep you grounded during uncertain times, helping you to focus on the "now" rather than what may or may not happen.

Mindfulness can create a distance between our thoughts, feelings, and reactions. In doing so, we can learn to observe our feelings of worry or distress without judgment. Being present means paying attention to what's happening right now, not letting stressful and troubling thoughts take over. Research shows that mindfulness, which involves being aware of your surroundings and body in the present, can offer a range of benefits.

Benefits of mindfulness include:

- improving your relationships with others;
- reducing stress;
- enhancing your ability to concentrate;
- helping to manage anxiety;

Additionally, being present can help you:

- savour pleasant experiences;
- pay attention to the people who matter to you;
- entirely focus on tasks or chores;
- think deeply while enjoying a book or movie;
- calm racing thoughts or overthinking;

Your body accompanies you in your daily routine every single day. It's possible to get up early, get to work, and take care of your obligations on your own.

Being present does not mean showing up to work on time and getting through the day; it means knowing what's on your mind at the moment. We all have our minds projected into the future or sometimes into the past; however, it should be a short journey. In every task you perform, your mind should be present. Being present means that your physical body and mind are focused on your work. Finding someone who can show you how powerful the present is can really make your life better. Living in the moment has numerous advantages. What's the point of focusing on the present moment? Because it contributes to your energy levels and motivation to achieve what you want and aspire for. The present makes you a better listener to your friends and increases your awareness. It can help you feel happier and appreciate what is around you.

Good habits for your future well-being are built when you practice the here and now. Stress and sudden mood changes are reduced by present-moment awareness over time because you have more control over your thoughts. Here are some tips to help you be more present in your daily life:

- focus on your breathing;
- practice meditation;
- limit the time you spend on social media;
- stay connected with your body;

- understand that you don't have all the answers;
- keep a gratitude journal.

4.8 Avoid multitasking

Many of us multitask for at least part of the time. While it may be tough to avoid entirely, it's a good idea to reflect on how we multitask. It's possible to hold a conversation while studying or updating an Excel spreadsheet. However, research shows that multitasking makes it harder to focus, regulate emotions, and remember important information. Sometimes, multitasking is fine; for example, you may find your morning commute more enjoyable if you listen to a podcast while driving. However, you may benefit from trying monotasking. Monotasking is when you focus on one activity at a time. This approach might help you when studying or working, as it allows you to be more present and attentive to what you're doing.

According to a study conducted by a university in London, sending emails or checking social media while talking on the phone lowers a person's IQ more significantly than losing a night's sleep, smoking cannabis, or watching hours of television. Multitasking can also have a significant impact on productivity. The time it takes to adjust to a new task is what happens when we keep switching tasks. Task-switching over time can reduce productivity by up to 40%, according to the American Psychological Association. Switching costs can add up to significant amounts when people switch tasks repeatedly, even though they may be relatively small. It could take more time and lead to more errors if you multitask.

4.9 Putting an end to limiting thoughts

If we want to change our subconscious programming, all the parts we've discussed so far are closely connected to one another.

When we talk about limiting thoughts, we're referring to thoughts that undermine our positivity, essentially, negative thoughts.

Negative thoughts can trigger several well-known clinical problems. Understanding how you think now and the issues that come with it is the key to changing your negative thoughts. How we feel and act is influenced by our thoughts, emotions, and behaviors. Therefore, even though we all have unhelpful thoughts occasionally, it's important to know what to do when they arise so they don't change the course of our day. Therapy can often help change negative thoughts, but you can also learn to change your thought patterns on your own. Some ways to get rid of negative thoughts are:

- Use mindfulness to become more aware.
- Identifying bad thoughts.
- Changing negative thoughts with more positive ones.
- Accepting negative thoughts instead of trying to ignore or ignore them.
- Understanding how to deal with feedback and criticism.
- Writing down your thoughts in a journal.

Suppose we want to reframe thoughts and present them positively. In that case, we're talking about a technique that allows us to notice the negative aspects of a situation and then look at them from a different perspective. Do you have a different perspective on this problem/situation? For example, you're tired of your role as a teacher. You have many student papers to correct, exam deadlines, and responsibilities, and you're exhausted to the point where you're not even sure you still enjoy your job. Now, how about tweaking some words and seeing how it sounds? Let's see how our thoughts would change if we read it positively.

Instead of feeling exhausted and unsure about your job, you might say to yourself, "There are challenging tasks to complete, and I don't feel comfortable handling all these activities and responsibilities. At this point, I start wondering if there are ways to delegate minor tasks to someone else, or I begin to think if there are less stringent deadlines to meet that still meet expectations." You can step back and observe if there is a different way of looking at things by reframing your words. You may notice a quick shift in your feelings by changing your thoughts, and eventually, you'll also see a change in your behaviour. We start paying attention to all the bad things that could happen because of fear, which leads to overthinking. However, once you've learned you're overthinking, you can stop and continue thinking about all the positive aspects. Spend as much time as possible thinking positively; even if this may seem like toxic positivity, it's simply allowing yourself to consider another option. With this technique, you'll find a middle ground regarding the situation, a more neutral way of looking at and expecting things. If you want to reinforce this way of acting, you can repeat your mantra, which we've seen as a strong encouragement to pursue and achieve our goals. Many different types of cognitive distortions contribute to negative thinking. The power of these negative thought patterns can be reduced by learning more about them and remembering that thoughts are not facts.

4.10 Don't talk about the past

Is it the right choice to let go of everything that doesn't make you feel good? Or how can one stop dwelling on past actions? Remember, our ability to recall the past is important, and we don't want to lose it because we would lose our capacity to learn from our mistakes and avoid repeating them.

The past can evoke intense emotions such as guilt and regret. These emotions can serve as a guide, showing us when we've strayed too far from our values. However, excessive rumination on the past leads to unproductive and circular thinking, trapping us in a cycle where our emotions become harmful rather than constructive. This can become overwhelming and toxic, causing us to feel out of control. Remembering that our thoughts do not define who we are is important. They do not always reflect our authentic selves or values, and we are not entirely responsible for the negative or distressing thoughts that enter our minds. The junk that pops up is normal. A study suggests that efforts to suppress specific thoughts only increase recurrence. Mantras like "stop thinking about it" or "just think of something positive" are ineffective and may even worsen our mood.. It's been suggested that attempting to control our thoughts reinforces them, making them stronger and more frequent. Therefore, the first step in not dwelling too much on the past is to cease trying to suppress those thoughts.

It is commonly believed that anxiety is usually associated with future events, while depression is linked to past experiences.

However, it's not unusual to experience anxiety from past situations and depression related to the future.

In short, our thoughts about the past can trigger any emotion: high-energy emotions like anxiety that push us to act or low-energy emotions like depression that discourage us from taking action.

Understanding this is crucial for battling our destructive impulses.

When we are anxious, our impulse is to move quickly, but it's better to try to slow down. And when we are depressed, the impulse is not to act, but it's probably better to get up and do something.

We must remember that all actions we take to leave the past behind us contribute to building our future, so all exercises we do for this purpose will help us enjoy the present.

What should we do, then, to forget the past?

To eliminate excessive thoughts related to the past, here are some practical exercises:

Focus on the present

Staying in the present can be very helpful for everyone, especially introverts who tend to be anxious and overthink their thoughts. Still deciding whether to start a meditation practice? There are many ways to ground yourself in the present moment.

Here are some ideas:

- Disconnect from social media and other forms of media. Spend time away from your computer or social media and try new activities. To find new inspiration, do this for a few days.

- Eat mindfully. Treat yourself to one of your favourite meals and savour every bite. Chew slowly and appreciate the flavours as if you had a culinary experience.

- Get outside. Even if it's only around your block, take a walk. You should pay attention to what you see, hear and smell.

Trying to forget

We all have some skeletons in our closet, whether it's a genuinely grotesque moment or an unpleasant memory. We all wish we could erase certain situations from our minds. Some memories fade, while others stay with you, like trauma. These memories are strong, and it feels like they drain you from within. They manifest in various ways, sometimes even as flashbacks that bring back bodily sensations you don't want to feel, from physical exhaustion to mental fatigue. While we all hope to live a happy and carefree life, putting this "mantra" into practice isn't so easy. Despite the darkness, there are still certain positive aspects that we can't forget. When you manage to control these past events that traumatised you and experience them as normal emotions, certainly much less intense than when you first lived them, you've made progress. This milestone doesn't just apply to trauma but to any past thought that has affected you in some way (even if it's just pure embarrassment). If you learn to manage these feelings, you will adopt a growth mindset that allows you to think about the future, grow, and experience all the facets of life.

Learn to forgive the most important person in your life: yourself

Transform your relationship with yourself into one that is kind and loving, free from judgment and self-criticism.

As a neutral spectator, observe a situation and become curious about what you're learning about yourself and what opportunities present themselves to you.

Embrace failure, disappointment, and inadequacies as opportunities for growth and development, and avoid being self-critical about your flaws.

What could this situation mean? Ask yourself questions. What lessons can I draw from this experience? What is the opportunity? What skills can I develop as a result of this situation? Taking care of yourself when things get tough helps you get better. However, many people are not compassionate with themselves. Dwelling on the past prevents you from letting go, and if you criticise yourself for something you've done, try to focus on forgiving yourself.

Here are some ways to start:

- Note down a stressful thought.
- The emotions and physical responses that arise should be monitored.

- Acknowledge that your feelings are real for you at this moment.
- Adopt a mantra like: "I can accept myself as I am" or "I am enough".

Self-compassion is a concept drawn initially from Buddhist psychology.

Buddhists fundamentally saw it as relating to oneself with kindness and compassion.

Self-compassion was operationally defined by Kristin Neff so that we could measure and study it.

Neff says: "Self-compassion is about relating to ourselves kindly, just as we are, flaws and all".

When one exhibits compassion, they can discern the distinction between making a wrong decision and being a negative person. You comprehend that your worth is not contingent upon a circumstance, a statement, or any thoughts you may have.

Neff outlines three key components of Self-Compassion:

- Self-kindness: treating ourselves with understanding, compassion, patience, empathy, and kindness (instead of being critical and judgmental).

- Recognising our shared humanity: feeling connected to others rather than isolated.

- Mindfulness: do not ignore your pain or exaggerate it. Instead, try to be realistic about what you're feeling.

According to Neff, you need all three of these characteristics to be genuinely compassionate with yourself.

Set some goals

One of the most effective ways to avoid dwelling on the past is to focus on the present and consider the future.

Setting goals gives your life a positive direction.

Are you unable to establish realistic objectives?

Setting challenging goals and achieving them is possible. Consider focusing on one goal at a time if you tend to overthink.

Here are some ways to plan your goals and ensure they suit you.

We recommend using a goal journal to define your goals' details, what to work on first, how you'll overcome challenges, and so on. You can get to work once your mind is in the right place. You could focus without distractions on a larger goal after achieving some more minor victories. Being distraction-free doesn't mean you don't need to take breaks. Do you want to grow and achieve some amazing life objectives, but don't know where to start? Writing down goals helps you stay on track and stay on track. Clarity, strategy, execution, and perseverance are the four essential ingredients for achieving your objectives. When you implement a plan that includes all these elements, even overthinkers can take action and achieve results:

- Goal setting (what + why) = clarity
- Goal planning (how) = strategy
- Motivation for action = execution
- Overcoming challenges = resilience

Goal journaling is a great way to focus your thoughts and prepare yourself for success. It helps you figure out what you really want, prioritize what comes first, and make an action plan.

Through the practice of goal journaling, individuals can establish precise objectives, identify the most significant objectives, subdivide them into manageable tasks, and even establish personal deadlines. One may also utilize it to monitor and visualize their progress over a period of time.

Practising goal journaling encourages you to reflect on your values and decide your goals. It can also aid in enhancing one's resilience to persist through challenging circumstances or obstacles.

Additionally, writing things down is a great way to organise your thoughts and prevent them from overwhelming your mind.

Finally, goal journaling can help you feel more confident about the goals you choose to set, as it allows you to consider the "why" behind each goal.

This could be the solution you've been searching for if you're an overthinker looking for a way to break free and achieve your goals.

Some objectives might be more challenging than others. The why will help you prioritize your goals and decide which one to focus on first.

Incorporating goal journaling into your life is a powerful practice that allows your thoughts to breathe.

It gives you the time and space to evaluate different approaches to your goals while providing a tangible view of the actions you need to take to achieve your long-term goals.

To get started, set small goals and feel free to change your approach if something isn't working as you'd like. During each journaling session, note the changes within yourself: the clarity, confidence, and strategic direction from taking time for yourself each day.

If necessary, start from scratch

If, despite trying all the techniques mentioned above, you have not been able to get rid of your negative thoughts and you find yourself dwelling on the past, unable to enjoy the present, and fearful of the future, it might be helpful to start from scratch.

Many people who live in toxic environments, surrounded by negative thoughts that affect their mental and physical health, struggle to improve their situation despite numerous attempts.

When all efforts prove futile, and no improvements are visible, a drastic change becomes necessary. This change allows us to leave the past behind and focus solely on our present and future.

Starting a new life and beginning from scratch is a powerful act. Leaving a job, a relationship or friends requires tremendous effort but can undoubtedly lead to great results. When we find ourselves in the right environment, we can finally release negative thoughts and start anew, concentrating on a brighter future.

Overthinking involves a cycle in which you revisit the same thoughts or worries without making progress. It has the potential to be exhausting and have an impact on both your sleep quality and your mental and physical well-being.

You can talk to others, find distractions, recognise triggers, and reassess your perspective to break this cycle.

If these suggestions don't help, consider seeking assistance from a mental health professional.

Even if you haven't found ways to feel better yet, don't worry! We have more practical exercises for you to try. We are all different, but we all share the same goal: to free ourselves from negative thoughts, stress, and anxiety.

Let's see if these exercises might work for you.

4.11 Include meditation in your daily activities

We all know what it's like to stay awake at night, dwelling on past decisions or worrying about present and future ones.

We can live with more peace and happiness by guiding ourselves toward clear actions that align with our potential by stopping overthinking.

When we engage in excessive thinking, we may experience a sense of immobility within our thoughts, entangled in a cycle of contemplation, unable to let go of the past, progress forward, or make decisions. Left unchecked, overthinking can lead to anxiety, depression, or mental disorders like obsessive-compulsive disorder.

Even in its mildest form, overthinking is not beneficial. The more we're stuck in our heads, the less connected we are to the wisdom in our bodies and hearts. When we let go of overthinking, we are guided by self-trust and confidence in our wise intuition.

Meditation can be the bridge that helps us transition from overthinking to simply being. When we're confidently connected to our true selves, we live in a state of greater clarity and have less need to overthink. Meditation brings this clarity to the forefront by strengthening the following qualities.

Through meditation, we become more aware of when we are overthinking. Observing our thoughts creates space between the thinker and the thought. Is overthinking helping me? Studies show that awareness of the thought process is often enough to stop rumination. Any meditation will help calm overthinking, but mindful meditation is a great place to start. Try just 10 minutes of meditation daily, sitting and observing your breath to reduce negative thoughts. Every time a thought intrudes, acknowledge it without judgment, then return to awareness of your breath. Observing the breath with a sense of joy, curiosity, or wonder can help you focus on the physical sensation of the breath. You'll start out thinking more than taking in your breath, but as your mind gets used to being instead of doing, this balance will shift. Whatever type of meditation you choose, carve out time for yourself, whether 10-20 minutes a day. Dress comfortably, sit with your hands on your knees, close your eyes, and start breathing; focus only on that. As mentioned earlier, thoughts may reappear, but over time and with the control of our mind through this practice, they will gradually fade away.

Guided meditation

A teacher leads guided meditation, either in person or via audio or video.

In the beginning, it's recommended that an expert guide you through the fundamental steps of meditation practice. Whenever we are trying to learn a new skill, it's important to have an experienced teacher whom we trust and can relate to. Having a guide is not just important; it's essential when exploring the complexities and subtleties of the mind.

Understanding what we're trying to accomplish through meditation is always a good place to start.

In traditional meditation, you are first taught how to visualise the contents of the mind and how best to approach different exercises so you know how to get the most out of the practice.

Then, you are taught how to meditate to become more proficient.

Learning how to replicate the calm and clarity developed during meditation in everyday life is the final step.

A guide or teacher explains the mind's inner workings and how it's likely to behave during meditation.

Meditation techniques and how to apply them to everyday life may be explained by the teacher.

Meditating alone

Unguided meditation (or solo meditation) allows the practitioner to customize how they wish to meditate independently, including duration, space, and level of silence. When contemplating on your own, you tend to do so without any aids from outside sources.

Find a quiet space with minimal interruptions first. A chair or the floor are usually a good place to sit. You should choose a posture that feels good to your body. Start by taking deep breaths and inhaling through your nose and exhaling through your mouth.

Meditating on their own without a guide explains the process. Visualisations, mantras, or body scans are some of the techniques a solo practitioner might use. If you're inexperienced, starting with guided meditation can be helpful if you're starting out.

Alternatively, some people may sit silently, paying attention to their bodies and thoughts.

For many, meditation is an excellent escape from the stresses of everyday life; for some, it helps promote better health and combat insomnia, while for others, it provides a safe space to retreat their minds away from the frantic pace of modern life. Regardless of one's role in life, it's a safe space to escape occasionally. Meditation carries the belief that the mind can either be emptied or find an escape from thoughts and problems. When we find ourselves in a safe harbor, we are predisposed to having better quality human relationships. This means that meditation, besides improving our mental and physical health, also enhances how we interact and, thus, our relationships. We cannot stop the mind from thinking because of its nature. Still, the real breakthrough lies in the ability to observe our thoughts as if we were external spectators, with detachment, so that they do not suck us into a vortex of discomfort and paranoia. When we practice meditation in any form, we focus on the present; at that moment, we train the mind to understand why we think and focus on a single goal: transforming our mind and perspective.

4.12 Finding solutions to our problems

Let's face it, dealing with problems can be challenging, sometimes leaving you feeling paralysed and out of control.

However, there are steps you can take to break down the issue and regain more control over it.

You can avoid insecurity and despair by tackling the issue proactively when you're at a crossroads or when you're struggling with a decision.

Focus on what you can do rather than things beyond your control, and feel satisfied that you've done your best, even if you haven't found a definitive solution to the problem.

You can use these basic steps to tackle problems one at a time:

- **Define the problem**. What exactly is happening? Sometimes, a problem seems too big to handle. However, it can seem more manageable if you create a list and break it down into smaller parts.

- **Set some goals**. Focus on the steps to resolve things rather than just thinking about what you wish would happen.

- **Brainstorm possible solutions.** Be creative and explore all the options that come to mind.

- **Exclude obvious and poor options.** Review your list of ideas and rule out those that are unrealistic or unhelpful.

- **Examine the consequences.** Look at the other choices and write down their advantages and disadvantages.

- **Identify the best solutions.** It's time to decide. Take a look at your options and pick the ones that are the most useful and practical.

- **Put your solutions into practice.** Have confidence in yourself and commit to trying one of your solutions.

After going through all the steps mentioned above, ask yourself how it went. If the solution you tried didn't work and you had other options, try another one before giving up.

4.13 How to proactively combat negative thoughts?

Our brains are wired to focus on negative thoughts and experiences, and we'll keep repeating that throughout this guide. This way of thinking helped our ancestors to stay safe and respond quickly to dangerous situations. When we get stuck in negative thought patterns, our brains generate more negative thoughts which then affect our bodies and behaviors. Given that our brains are wired this way, how can we effectively deal with our negative thoughts? It's important to focus on managing negative thoughts rather than trying to eliminate them. Our brains are designed to think; we don't want to stop that. Instead, we want to learn how to turn those negative thoughts into positive ones and be more compassionate with ourselves. Below, we will elaborate on **the 3-question technique** developed to help eliminate negative thoughts.

Question 1: Is the thought I'm having real, meaning, is there evidence to support it?

Don't let negative thoughts control your life and dictate how things should unfold.

It may not be easy to switch to positive thoughts immediately, but you can consistently challenge negative ones with these three questions. Thoughts are uncontrollable; they are generated by our minds and shaped by our circumstances or experiences. We tend to think things that aren't grounded in actuality. Evaluate the veracity of the proof we use to back up these ideas to dismiss them. Thoughts are not facts; some may be, but even those are usually open to interpretation and perception, while most are not based on reality and are products of our minds dwelling on the past or dreading the future. Giving ourselves a bit of distance with the questions we encounter enables us to scrutinise our thoughts and emotions. It gives us much more influence over our feelings (and, as a result, our lives) than we may have previously realised.

Question 2: Is this thought helpful?

Our brains constantly generate new thoughts from complex processes influenced by our current mental state, emotions, brain chemistry, environment, previous thoughts, memories, short-term memory, and more.

Thoughts may seem random because our minds sometimes combine unrelated ideas, producing creative results. By observing our thoughts, we can better manage our time and energy. Instead of accepting unhelpful thoughts as reality and feeling unhappy, we can reject or ignore them. For example, thinking that you're a loser doesn't help, so it's a thought we need to discard immediately.

Question 3: Do I feel good about this thought?

The last question we need to ask ourselves is the most important one. Always remember that thoughts are just thoughts; we can give them a negative or positive spin. We're here to understand how to free our minds, so how do we feel when we face specific thoughts? Notice how this thought makes you sad, angry, jealous, hurt, afraid, etc. What would the experience be like if you let go of this thought? Imagine that thought leaving you and your mind. How would your mental state change? By asking these questions, you can observe the internal cause and effect of specific thoughts. You may notice that believing a thought creates a disturbance, ranging from mild discomfort to fear to panic.

As we often try to push away negative thoughts, it's important to ask ourselves how we feel in the presence of specific thoughts or how we would feel if we let those thoughts leave our minds. The questions we ask ourselves not only help us understand if an idea is essential and should be retained but also make us reflect clearly on our minds and what might be harmful to us. If you find this technique practical, we suggest keeping it handy and using it whenever you think it might be helpful.

In addition to the technique mentioned, all the teachings and information provided in this guide are essential for better understanding our minds, what influences us, and how we can free our heads from excessive and negative thoughts or give them a positive spin.

This guide has highlighted various techniques for dealing with mental discomfort, anxiety, stress, and excessive thoughts, from guided or solo meditation to the 3-question technique to mantras.

Everyone is free to choose the method they prefer to completely free themselves from this whirlwind of thoughts and return to being happy, with a focus on the future and the goals we've set for ourselves.

If we can't find ourselves again, we've seen that it might be helpful to start from scratch. This is not cowardice but a choice that, in some situations, may be inevitable to regain control of our minds.

Let's take back our freedom.

Conclusion

Research shows that, on average, people generate more than 6,000 thoughts daily.

While it's common to be distracted by unwanted or occasional thoughts, excessive thinking is not easily dismissed.

It becomes difficult to focus on anything else because of these thoughts.

The desire to analyze situations and consider all possible outcomes is natural. A new reality that is often negative and unproductive can be created when overthinking becomes a habit. Overthinking can also create a new reality that is positive and transformative.

How we perceive and react to things is influenced by how we think. When we overthink, we tend to focus on negative possibilities, often creating a more stressful, anxious, and overwhelming reality than it should be. We can create a new reality that is empowering and transformative when we learn to control our thoughts and focus on the good things in life. This new reality is a product of our imagination and a mindset we can cultivate and develop. Our lives are influenced by thoughts. Athletes, for instance, frequently resort to imagining themselves achieving their objectives. By visualising success, they create a new reality in their minds that can help them perform better in real life.

Positive thinking and visualisation are often attributed to successful people.

But how can we cultivate this new reality through overthinking? We must act on our intricate webs and frameworks of thought.

We can step back and reframe our thoughts when we catch ourselves overthinking and focusing on the negative. Instead of focusing on what is the worst thing that could happen, we can ask ourselves what is the best thing that could happen. This simple shift in perspective can change the entire trajectory of our thoughts and create a more optimistic reality.

Another way to cultivate a new reality through overthinking is to focus on solutions rather than problems.

We get stuck in a cycle of analyzing the situation and fretting about possible outcomes when we overthink.

However, if we focus on finding solutions, we can create a more proactive and solution-oriented reality.

Overthinking can help us better understand ourselves and our values, which can lead to a new reality. When we overthink, we often analyse our thoughts and beliefs in depth.

This can help you become more aware of yourself and figure out what really matters.

Thinking too much can be both good and bad.

The habit can lead to a hostile and unproductive reality. The positive aspects of a situation can be created when we learn to control our thoughts and focus on them.

We can create a new reality by changing our thought patterns, focusing on solutions, and understanding ourselves better.

People often use unhealthy coping mechanisms to deal with these situations, such as social isolation and compulsive behaviour.

Fortunately, you can learn to stop overthinking and prevent intrusive thought patterns from taking over your life.

Our mental health and overall well-being can be impacted by thinking too much in this guide.

We have also discussed how to identify and overcome overthinking habits so you can start living a more relaxed and fulfilling life.

We found out that thinking too much is a common issue that affects people from all walks of life. It can cause anxiety, stress, and depression, as well as impact our physical health.

The good news is that it's possible to let go of thinking too much and live a happier life.

Next, we explored some of the most common causes of overthinking, including past trauma, fear of failure, and perfectionism.

Understanding the underlying causes of our overthinking helps us tackle them and develop better thinking habits. We then discussed some practical strategies for overcoming overthinking, including meditation and positive self-talk. These techniques can help us stay in the present moment, challenge negative thoughts, and cultivate a more positive outlook on life and the future. We talked about taking care of ourselves and being kind to ourselves. We discovered that taking care of ourselves is crucial for our physical and mental health. Getting enough sleep, eating well, and working out regularly are some of the things you need to do. It's about being kind to ourselves and treating ourselves the same way we'd treat a buddy. The journey to stop overthinking can be challenging but worth it. First, remember that change takes time. Breaking a habit that has been a part of your life for a long time is not easy and won't happen overnight. But if you persevere, you will get there. You should celebrate every small step you take toward overcoming overthinking. No matter how small it seems, every step counts. Secondly, remind yourself of the benefits of stopping overthinking. When you stop overthinking, you will have more mental clarity, less stress, and a greater sense of peace. You will also become more aware and capable of making the right decisions and enjoying life more. As you work to stop overthinking, keep these benefits in mind as you keep these benefits in mind. It's not your fault if you've developed this habit, many people struggle with overthinking, and it's not your fault if you've developed it. Be gentle and patient instead of beating yourself up. Remember that you are making progress, and that's what matters. Finally, surround yourself with supportive people. People who understand what you're going through and encourage you can make a big difference in your journey to stop overthinking.

You can seek support from friends and family, talk to a therapist or counselor, or confide in a trusted friend or counselor.

In conclusion, the journey to stop overthinking is not easy but worth undertaking.

Be patient with yourself, take baby steps, remember the good stuff, and surround yourself with people who love you. You can overcome overthinking and start living a more fulfilling life.

By reading this guide, you have taken the first step toward freeing yourself from the cycle of worry, doubt, and anxiety.

As you prepare to put what you've learned into practice, here are some thoughts to help you on your journey.

First, remember that overcoming overthinking is a process. There are setbacks and it won't happen overnight.

It's all about staying focused and moving forward. Every small step you take to break the habit of overthinking counts.

Next, be patient with yourself. When you feel like you're not making progress fast enough, it's easy to feel frustrated or discouraged. But remember that change takes time. Be kind to yourself, celebrate your successes, and don't beat yourself up for your mistakes.

Finally, remember to practice self-compassion. I will never tire of repeating this!

It's important not to scold or judge yourself harshly if you overthink. You should show yourself the same compassion and understanding you would show a friend. You should treat yourself with the same care and compassion you would give to someone you love.

Overthinking is a common issue affecting millions worldwide (I don't know how often we've said this, but I hope it's clear). Don't feel like you're the only one dealing with this affliction, don't feel like you're the only one.

You are not weak or flawed.

You can reach out to family, friends, or a therapist for help. You don't have to face this alone. Remember that life is meant to be enjoyed. Don't let your thoughts get in the way of enjoying life. Practice mindfulness, stay present, and savour the small pleasures in life. Eliminate the burden of excessive thought from your mind. The concept suggests changing our thoughts can change our experiences and create a better life. To change our thoughts, we need to become aware of them and challenge any negative or limiting beliefs. To cultivate a positive mindset, we can reframe our thoughts and focus on positive affirmations.

Changing our thoughts can lead to more happiness, stronger connections, and a healthier you. Adopting a growth mindset and focusing on the good can make our lives more fulfilling and prosperous. Our thoughts are powerful and can shape our lives in meaningful ways. They influence our emotions, behaviours, and, ultimately, our outcomes. There are negative emotions such as anxiety, stress, and depression that can be caused by negative thoughts, while positive emotions can be caused by positive thoughts.

To change our thoughts, we must become aware of them and challenge any negative or limiting beliefs. This means being mindful of our self-talk and recognising when negative thoughts or self-talk arise. By doing so, we can reframe our thoughts and focus on positive affirmations, visualisation, and gratitude to cultivate a more positive mindset. Saying good things about ourselves or our situation is called positive affirmations. Visualisation involves imagining ourselves achieving our goals and experiencing success in our minds. Gratitude means noticing the good things in our life and saying thank you for them. By changing our thoughts and cultivating a positive mindset, we can experience various benefits. These include heightened contentment, stronger connections, and overall well-being. Being positive can make us stronger and more resilient when things go wrong. A growth mindset involves a willingness to learn, grow, and embrace new experiences. We can transform our lives by changing our thoughts. A willingness to challenge ourselves and commitment are required. Become aware of our thoughts and actively work to change them to create a more positive and fulfilling life. I recommend reading this guide more than once, as the techniques for solving the problem of overthinking may take time to truly sink in. Be kind to yourself, live in the moment, and take care of yourself. You are worthy of it!

Final Acknowledgements

Thank you for choosing to read my book. I hope it has been an exciting and inspiring experience for you. If you found the book helpful and appreciated its content, I would be grateful if you could leave feedback on Amazon. Your encouraging comments have always been a great support to me and have helped me grow as a writer.

If you have any inquiries or apprehensions regarding any aspect of the book, please do not hesitate to contact me via email. I am open to your opinions and constructive criticism, which allows me to improve my work and better meet your needs as readers.

Email Address: Amoslloyd2023@gmail.com

I sincerely appreciate your time and effort in reading my book. Again, I appreciate your help and am looking forward to hearing your thoughts.

Printed in Great Britain
by Amazon